THE SONG JESUS SINGS

....

DRAWING NEAR TO THE HEART
OF GOD THROUGH THE
SONG OF SONGS

JOEL RATCLIFFE

Transforming Books
ADELAIDE, SOUTH AUSTRALIA

Copyright © 2018 by Joel Ratcliffe.

All rights reserved. No part of this publication may be reproduced, distributed or transmitted in any form or by any means, including photocopying, recording, or other electronic or mechanical methods, without the prior written permission of the publisher, except in the case of brief quotations embodied in critical reviews and certain other noncommercial uses permitted by copyright law. For permission requests, write to the publisher, at the address below.

Transforming Books
www.transformingbooks.com
info@transformingbooks.com

Cover art by Julie-Anne Powell
https://brushledartbyjulieanne.bigcartel.com/

Author photo by Nathan de la Garde

Unless otherwise noted, Scripture quotations are from the ESV® Bible (The Holy Bible, English Standard Version®), copyright © 2001 by Crossway, a publishing ministry of Good News Publishers. Used by permission. All rights reserved.

The Song Jesus Sings ~ Drawing near to God through the Song of Songs / Joel Ratcliffe. -- 1st ed.
ISBN 978-0-9953659-2-6

For the Hwang family, who gave so much to see Christ birthed in me.

Acknowledgements: *Steve Hwang, Mike Bickle, Peter Foote, Reuben Rose, Jono Ko, Sandy Hart and Simon Woodley have all made significant contributions to this book. I am so thankful for their input.*

What a deep well of inspiration! Such an interesting, refreshing and alluring way into the greatest of all songs. Joel Ratcliffe's first book (The Song Jesus Sings) draws from his rich personal experience of finding God in the wilderness and in the secret place. Full of the finest jewels and the richest nuggets, Joel unveils the beauty of God and His passionate desire for the Bride to walk in the fullness of her destiny.... challenging and inviting us to go deeper.
It is an experiential life manual providing the reader with joyful hope and practical spiritual tools necessary to walk and overcome every obstacle in their journey with our Bridegroom King.
Thank you Joel for making the Shulamite's journey your own. The body of Messiah and the prayer movement are so much richer for it!

Glenn Rowbotham
Senior Pastor & Director
Daylesford House of Prayer, Australia
Elohim House of Prayer, Mt Carmel, Israel.
www.elohimhouse.org

"Joel Ratcliffe is a young man with a heart for intimacy with Jesus. In this book, which could be used as daily readings, he expresses this in a well written and warm manner. He draws on many scriptural examples as he uses the "Song of Solomon" as a back drop. I gladly endorse the value of Joel's book."
- Rev Barry Manuel, Co-Pastor Healinglife Church, Adelaide.

"*In this book Joel has provided his intimate personal journey and 'journal' with our Loving Christ. You'll be encouraged with Scriptures and tips to venture into your personal and corporate love journey with our Intimate God. Enjoy!*"
-Pastor Toh Ng, Marion Vineyard Church, Adelaide

This has been such a refreshing and challenging journey through Song of Songs! As Joel uncovers the layers of this love song one can experience the depth of love and longing God has for His people. Joel has given insight and application in a way that leads to a greater understanding and connection to the heart of God - a life changing journey worth taking.
Coralie Preston - Director of WEC Australia

I first met Joel Ratcliffe in 2012 while speaking in the ACTS SCHOOL AT IHOP KC where he was a student. Later I met him a number of times in Sydney where he played a key role in the establishment of SYDNEY HOUSE OF PRAYER. Joel and I have had many many conversations in which I have found him not just to have a great understanding of the key values of the HOP movement but, I have also found him to be a clear communicator of those values. This, I believe is because he lives out these values. I believe this book will become a valuable resource and inspiration not just for those who are called into the HOP movement but for those called into the greater Prayer Movement.

Glen Vines.
Director of Lion's Roar House of Prayer & Strategic Warfare Intercessory Network.
Brisbane, Australia.

CONTENTS

Introduction..1
Value 1: The heart of the song.................................. 13
Value 2: The beauty of longing...............................29
Value 3: The divine kiss.. 45
Value 4: Weak yet lovely to God............................63
Value 5: Eating the fruit of Jesus' work................ 87
Value 6: An inheritance for Jesus........................... 97
Value 7: The infinite worth of a lovesick heart.............. 113
Value 8: Nothing shall separate us........................ 127
Value 9: Beauty bestowed....................................... 143
Value 10: The fellowship of His suffering........................ 155
Value 11: What to do with suffering.................................. 169
Value 12: There is more! 185
Value 13: Intercession and the return of the King......... 201
Conclusion... 217
Note 1: An outline of the Song of Solomon.....................223
Note 2: A paraphrase of the Song of Solomon..............227
Note 3: Understanding the language of the
 Song of Solomon.. 249

INTRODUCTION

AWAKE AUSTRALIA

God is up to something! From the Middle East to the Americas, Africa and New Zealand I have seen it with my own eyes. He is moving across the earth on a scale never seen before.

This book is written to provide some language and understanding to what I have seen. To add a voice of agreement from Australia, this great South land at the ends of the earth. It serves to call God's people to press into the deep things of His heart. For too long we have dabbled in the superficial and popular. Many have become disillusioned, apathetic. Yet there are those whom God has marked, hidden away and set apart for such a time as this. Often the ones who have been rejected, hurt and misunderstood by the institutional church. The enemy has planned to silence and separate the very ones God

INTRODUCTION

wants to use to bring His Church through the glory and the crisis about to crash upon planet earth.

This book is written in answer to the deep heart cry: *There must be more to following Jesus than this!* It is written to bring hope to hearts and as a reminder that God has not forsaken us. The time has come for my nation to awake and for yours too. King Jesus is calling us forth!

HOW TO READ THIS BOOK

The subject of this book is controversial. It serves as a guide into the Song of Songs. In our time the Holy Spirit is reawakening an ancient understanding of this little, mostly forgotten book and using it to lead His people into the deep things of God's heart. The book has, for the last 200 years or so, been primarily interpreted as a poetic picture of the love between a man and woman (*The Bible and Us: A priest and a Rabbi read Scripture Together*, Andrew M. Greeley and Jacob Neusner, 1990, p. 34) Yet, would it surprise you to know it is traditionally read each year at the Jewish Celebration of Passover. Passover celebrates the beginning of God saving His people from slavery in Egypt and taking them on the journey of making them His covenant people (*Why do we sing the Song of Songs at Passover*, Scolnic, 1996). The Jewish people for millennia have understood the Song of Songs to be a picture of the love relationship between God and His people.

The Song of Songs has three main characters: the bride, the Bridegroom and the daughters of Jerusalem. The book tells the story of the deepening love relationship between the bride (us –both individually and corporately) and the Bridegroom (Jesus). The bride starts in immature love and the book traces the highs and lows of relationship until the bride comes up from the wilderness fully mature as a partner suitable for Jesus (Genesis 2:18 and Ephesians 4:13). The daughters of Jerusalem serve to provide commentary on the dialogue between the bride and Bridegroom. They represent young, immature believers who are touched and influenced by a person who pursues God wholeheartedly. These immature believers are eventually moved by what they observe to enter into the same journey.

The purpose of this book is not to provide a verse by verse or comprehensive explanation or commentary of the Song of Songs. Rather it is meant to give enough of an explanation and interpretation to give readers the tools to go deep into the truths of the Song of Songs for themselves. It is meant to give a little taste of the depth and beauty of God to be found in the Song of Songs.

The book is divided into 13 chapters or "values", each of which focuses on one step of the journey. At the end of each chapter, there is a practical exercise to help you pursue that chapter's value in a deeper way. I recommend at least reading through these exercises as they open the way to receiving revelation on that value for yourself.

In short, this book is meant to not only be read, but experienced. It is not designed to be read as you would normally read a book. It's not meant to be consumed from cover to cover in a sitting. It is meant to be read slowly, meditated upon, thought about and combined with a thorough examination of scripture. Through it, my hope is that you would make a resolution to go deep into the study and meditation of the Song of Songs for yourself.

Finally, before you progress past this introduction and into Value 1 I recommend flipping to the Outline and Paraphrase of the Song of Songs in the Notes section as well as reading through the Song of Songs itself to gain a basic understanding of the book's storyline. This will allow you to gain the best understanding of the rest of this book.

The Song Jesus Sings

A HOUSE OF PRAYER FOR ALL NATIONS

You may now be wondering, why write about the Song of Songs? And, what significance does it have to play in our time?

In recent years, across the body of Christ worldwide, there has been an increasing emphasis on prayer. This has also been true of the Australian Church. Prayer meetings are springing up both within the organisational schedules of churches and in the daily lives (e.g. workplaces, homes and universities) of believers around the country. Younger Christians are beginning to pray. No longer are prayer meetings the exclusive domain of older women who labour faithfully for years behind closed doors. Rather the Holy Spirit is calling the whole Church to pray and believers, young and old, are responding.

As well as an increase in prayer within the institutional church, there is a growing movement across the earth to establish Houses of Prayer (in many different expressions): separate organisations focused on establishing communities of day and night intercession.

One of the key ministries in this movement has been the International House of Prayer, Kansas City

(IHOP-KC). Birthed in 1999 and led by Pastor Mike Bickle, IHOP-KC has in many ways led this movement and served as an inspiration for the birthing of similar prayer ministries around the world. In 1984, it was estimated there were fewer than 25 ministries on the earth whose primary mission was to establish places where worship and intercession arose before God 24/7 (*Growing in Prayer*, Mike Bickle, 2014, ch.28). Fast forward 30 years to 2014 and it is now estimated there are over 10,000 ministries whose primary mission is this goal (*Growing in Prayer*, Mike Bickle, 2014, ch.28). Surely this can only be seen as a move of the Holy Spirit.

As we observe the Holy Spirit calling believers globally to pray, we must ponder in our hearts: why? Why is God emphasising the importance of prayer? Why is God raising up places of prayer separate to the institutional church model in place for centuries? The answers are both glorious and sobering.

WHAT IS GOD GETTING AT?

As a member of staff at the Sydney House of Prayer I spent three years, 4-6 hours a day, in prayer, worship and study of the Word. I often (at least weekly) ponder the circumstances of my life. I wonder why I apparently wasted my youth on what many consider a trivial and pointless pursuit. Yet, what the Lord has highlighted to me is that the circumstances of my life mean nothing apart from the context of one great spiritual reality. This reality is the consummation (i.e. the completion) of the gospel of Jesus Christ. In short, the gospel of Jesus Christ is the story of the glorious, uncreated God, and His great longing to dwell with His people. This longing is like the longing of a bridegroom for his bride.

LONGING FOR A BRIDE

Throughout the Bible, God uses the metaphor of marriage to describe His covenant relationship with His people.

"For your Maker is your husband, the LORD of hosts is his name" (Isaiah 54:5a)

In the gospel of John (3:27 - 29), John the Baptist describes his ministry to prepare the way for Jesus as being like the friend (best man) of a bridegroom.

"John answered, "A person cannot receive even one thing unless it is given him from heaven. You yourselves bear me witness, that I said, 'I am not the Christ, but I have been sent before him.' The one who has the bride is the

INTRODUCTION

bridegroom. The friend of the bridegroom, who stands and hears him, rejoices greatly at the bridegroom's voice. Therefore this joy of mine is now complete."

In Revelation 19, an angel describes Jesus, the Lamb of God, as a bridegroom returning to marry His bride, the Church. If you will look for it, it is everywhere in scripture! Right at this minute in heaven, the burning desire of Jesus' heart is this: 'Is it time yet? How long, Father? Father, when is the day of my wedding? When do I get to return to my people?' Like a young man who longs for the day he will meet his bride and does not know when it will come, so Jesus waits in heaven, longing, desiring, looking forward. Matthew 24:36 makes it clear that like the young man who waits, so Jesus also waits not knowing the day nor the hour. Rather, Jesus lives to intercede for us. I believe His intercession goes something like this: *"Father, I desire that they also, whom you have given me, may be with me where I am..."* (John 17: 24)

Yet today, much like in the days when Jesus walked the earth 2000 years ago, there are so few who mourn or fast for the coming of the Bridegroom (Matthew 9:15). Instead, many Christians are primarily concerned with other things - careers and investments, entertainment, social lives and status, children, families, weddings and retirement plans.

Certainly, none of these things are wrong in and of themselves but when we honestly look at the lives of the apostles after Jesus' ascension, it is plain our lives are meant to be lived longing for our Lord's return. For the first century Church the return of Jesus was their 'blessed hope' (see Titus 2:13, 1 Peter 1:3-9 and *Christ's return: Our blessed hope, Lofquist, 2005*). His return and preparing for His return was what gave their lives context and purpose. They were sojourners longing for a better home with eyes fixed and lives focused on what is to come (Hebrews 11:13-16). Yet to the 21st century Church a pertinent question would be: How is it so few of us know or care about the desire of Jesus' heart to return? Where are the friends of the Bridegroom who would fast and pray until He comes? What bride who is engaged to a husband does not long for the day of her wedding? In a world of great injustices this is the greatest injustice on the planet. It is for this reason that God is raising up a prayer movement across the earth.

Jesus is longing for a people after His own heart and prayer is the means to this end. He is looking for people who would draw close to Him. He is looking for brothers and sisters who don't just pray more but pray what is on His heart because they care about what He cares about because they know Him deeply and intimately. This is true intercession. The question God is asking those who call themselves Christians right now is this: 'Who will separate themselves from the world to truly be my friends?' God is looking for sold-out-lovers who will give everything for Him because they have been wholly captured and consumed by His fiery, passionate desire for them.

Until the global Bride of Christ cries out, *"Come, Lord Jesus!"* (Revelation 22:20) Jesus is not returning because how can a bridegroom marry an unwilling bride? Thus, if the Holy Spirit really is raising up a body of praying believers who are close to His heart, with an understanding of His will and desire to be with His people, it is a sign on the earth of one thing and one thing alone: the return of Jesus grows near.

This is the reality which gives the circumstances of my life, the long hours in the prayer room and all the giving up of so many other valid pursuits, context, meaning and value.

AFTER HIS HEART

How then do we gain a revelation of God's heart? How do we come to a place where we are so captured by His desire for us that we will stand even like the saints in Revelation 12: 11 who *"... loved not their lives even unto death"*? How is it we become a bride who is crying out, *"Come, Lord Jesus, Come!"*

The answer is found in Psalm 84: 5-7:

"Blessed are those whose strength is in you, in whose heart are the highways to Zion. As they go through the Valley of Baca they make it a place of springs; the early rain also covers it with pools. They go from strength to strength; each one appears before God in Zion."

It is an ancient pilgrimage, a heart set on journeying toward heaven (Zion), that we must go on. It is a difficult journey yet glorious beyond words. This is the path Christ Himself told us we must follow:

"And he said to all, "If anyone would come after me, let him deny himself and take up his cross daily and follow me."" (Luke 9:23, 24)

Notice the point of this journey though. It is 'to save your life.' Though it involves taking up one's cross and losing one's life, the point is joy and true life forever. It is not a journey reserved for those who are spiritually elite or extreme. This is the journey all must take who would stand at the judgement seat on the final day and be told: *"...Well done, good and faithful servant..."*. (Matthew 25:23)

For comfort and understanding of this journey, the Holy Spirit is highlighting the ancient understanding of the Song of Solomon. Today, God is

INTRODUCTION

calling His people to once more understand this book in the same way ancient Israel did - as a book describing the love of God for His people and the journey a person goes on as they walk deeper into experiencing God's heart.

My prayer is that through the Song of Songs you would be captured by the desire of God for you, your family, friends and nation and a great cry would arise from Australia, this barren land at the ends of the earth: *"...glory to the righteous One!* (Isaiah 24: 16) *Come, Lord Jesus!"* (Revelation 22: 20).

Jesus is a Bridegroom King, He's coming soon... and we need to get ready!

VALUE ONE

....

THE HEART OF THE SONG

To go deep into the Song of Songs we need a lens to see through. We need a perspective from which to interpret what God was getting at when He authored these eight glorious chapters in the heart of Solomon. In other words, we need to set a goal of what to look for and focus on as we study. For example, we could choose to study for the purpose of figuring out the meaning of all the symbols and how the story flows together. But while it's important to understand the symbols and the basic story line there is so much more to the book than these. To gain this lens, this perspective, we must start on the rocky, yellow hills around Bethlehem, 3000 years ago.

In those days a young shepherd boy tended the sheep of his father in rain and snow, winter and summer, under the blazing sun, the shining moon and the myriad of stars about which he wrote so profoundly. Bethlehem was a forgotten little town then - out of the way and out of the consciousness of a troubled nation.

The job of shepherding was a menial and lonely task usually reserved for servants. Yet here was the eighth son of a wealthy citizen forgotten on the hills for months at a time. Yet it was amongst the sheep that God found him on the greatest day of his father, Jesse's, life.

1 Samuel 16 describes the reason for this day. Having rejected Israel's first King, Saul, God commanded the old prophet, Samuel, to fill his horn with oil and go to the town of Bethlehem. He was to anoint a new king from among the sons of Jesse. Down through the ages, the words of God about this task thunder with significance. *"...I have provided for MYSELF a king among his sons."* (1 Samuel 16:1 – emphasis added)

As the Bible tells, the elders of Bethlehem were afraid at the coming of the aged prophet. They wondered in fear at what fierce judgement Israel's last judge was coming to pronounce upon their humble town (1 Samuel 16:4). Samuel replied that he came in peace only to make a sacrifice and meet the man Jesse and his family. The ways of a prophet are mysterious the elders must have reasoned. If God had told him to make a sacrifice in Bethlehem and dine with this citizen, then it was blessing for the town. Accordingly, we find Samuel at Jesse's table, meeting his sons and enquiring of the Lord in his heart about the identity of God's chosen one.

Eliab, the eldest son, is the first to be introduced. Tall, dark, strong and handsome, he is a warrior. Samuel jumps ahead of God.

"Surely the Lord's anointed...!" he proclaims (1 Samuel 16:6).

I can imagine Eliab thrust out his chest. 'YES! I knew this day would come,' he thought. Jesse beamed with pride. And then the story took a most unexpected turn. God thundered from heaven through the old prophet's spirit. 'NO!

"Do not look on his appearance or on the height of his stature, because I have rejected him." (1 Samuel 16:7a)

'We've been down this path before Samuel. Don't you remember what happened with Saul? He was head and shoulders above the rest of his people and yet he failed completely to know, love and serve me.' (see 1 Samuel 10:23)

"For the LORD sees not as man sees: man looks on the outward appearance, but the LORD looks on the heart." (1 Samuel 16:7)

Samuel is bemused. He moves to meet the next brother, Abinadab. But God has not chosen him either. Shammah is next. "Nope," says Samuel. The next four brothers are not named by scripture but none of them are chosen either and now Samuel is confused.

He turns to Jesse and asks, *"Are these all the sons you have?"* (1 Samuel 16:11)

As we read this passage we can almost feel Jesse squirm. 'Well, you know, there is another one, the youngest. Little David. But no one really takes him seriously.

The New King James translation of this passage makes it clear that they could actually see David from where they stood.

The prophet was now incredulous, *"Send and get him, for we will not sit down until he arrives."* (1 Samuel 16:11)

When David was brought before Samuel the Lord spoke once again and this time it was the gentle, still whisper Samuel knew so well.

"Arise, anoint him, for this is he." Then Samuel took the horn of oil and anointed him in the midst of his brothers. And the Spirit of the LORD rushed upon David from that day forward. (1 Samuel 16:12, 13)

The Song Jesus Sings

GOD REVEALS HIS HEART

I believe this story marks the recorded beginning of David's revelation regarding the significance of the beauty of the Lord. By 'the beauty of the Lord' I don't only mean the physical appearance of God, the overwhelming beauty coming from the throne room in heaven, the thunder and lightning flashing on the sea of glass (Revelation 4). I mean the beauty of God's heart, the beauty of His emotional make-up, the beauty of His ways and His character, the beauty of the way He thinks and feels and deals with His people (His affections towards us). When we call a person we know beautiful, most often we are not only talking about physical appearance. We're talking about their character.

In the same way, the beauty of the Lord is that which we find most attractive about Him. While God Himself is the definition of beauty, each of us individually perceive different aspects of who He is and therefore find different parts of Him beautiful. The beauty of the Lord then is not something we can take hold of and necessarily define. Rather, the beauty of the Lord includes those aspects of God which take hold of us and captivate our hearts.

Here is David, the last son of a family who lives in the back hills of the Judean countryside. Nothing exciting ever happens in Bethlehem. And now the Bill Johnson, president of the nation, number one famous guy in the land comes to visit. The prophet wants to dine with David's family and David is left out, forgotten in the hills doing a menial task meant for servants. Couldn't someone have been sent to tend the sheep for those few hours Samuel visited? Is it safe to conclude David's family held contempt for him?

Yet while David's family might have written him off, God knew where he was. Even while the greatest prophet the nation had ever known was admiring tall, dark and handsome, God thundered from heaven and said, 'NO. I don't see as a man sees. I evaluate very differently. If you judge Jesse's sons by anything you can see with your eyes you're going to miss what I see.' Oh the beauty of God's heart! To see the weak ones, the forgotten ones, the ones who by man's standards don't qualify. He says, 'I see you, I know you, I choose you.' Friends, this is our story. Though you may be written off by many, God evaluates you by very different criteria.

I believe this experience became the foundation of David's identity. As Samuel retold this story to David over the years (as he undoubtedly became a mentor to the young man) the truth of God's character in seeing David, knowing him and choosing him out of obscurity served as a powerful affirmation of what David was doing when God called him. It affirmed in him the validity in God's eyes of what he was doing and what was in his heart.

THE MAN AFTER GOD'S OWN HEART

So, what was in David's heart? What was he doing on that fateful day Samuel visited? On this day, as on the other days he spent with the sheep, he was lost in the pursuit of knowing and loving God. He was lost in this pursuit because of the indescribable delight and pleasure he found in it. His life dream on those hills of Bethlehem had become (and continued to be for the rest of his life) this: to be filled with delight as he pursued and encountered the fiery, passion of God's heart for him. On the hills of Bethlehem, in the midst of what most would call mundane: standing with the sheep by day; singing songs to pass the long, lonely nights, God had revealed his heart. David became completely addicted to the delight of the experience. It is a question worth pondering: Are joy and delight the primary motivators of your relationship with God? Because this is what God has and intends for us.

So how do we know David was a man consumed with pursuing the delight that comes from encountering the beauty of God? Here are some examples.

Firstly, Psalm 8:3-4 – *"When I look at your heavens, the work of your fingers, the moon and the stars, which you have set in place, what is man that you are mindful of him, and the son of man that you care for him?"* David is on the lonely hills at night with the sheep and he is marveling at the majesty and power of God as revealed through the moon and the stars above him.

Secondly, Psalm 29:3 - *"The voice of the LORD is over the waters; the God of glory thunders, the LORD, over many waters."* David is again on the hills with the sheep. This time he's caught in a thunderstorm and he's encountering the power of God in the thunder and lightning.

Further along in his life, Psalm 60:4-5 records David praying. In the midst of war with Babylon (Mesopotamia) and Syria with crisis facing the nation, David gets lost in prayer and calls himself 'God's beloved one'.

"You have set up a banner for those who fear you, that they may flee to it from the bow. Selah. That your beloved ones may be delivered, give salvation by your right hand and answer us!"

He didn't call himself God's servant even though he used this phrase in the Psalms at other times

(Psalm 119:23 and 125; Psalm 116: 16; Psalm 86:16; Psalm 143:12). But here he called himself, 'God's beloved one'. I can imagine one of his friends overheard him and said, 'God's going to deliver who?' And David would have opened his eyes and said, 'Oh...oh yeah...people don't talk like this do they?' This was an entirely new understanding for people then – that God actually had deep affections for His people.

David was different from those of his generation. He had a different spirit and a different heart. He was on a journey which started by encountering God in the beauty of nature and moved deeper into encountering God's own affections toward him. Psalm 69: 8-10 describes the consequences of this:

"I have become a stranger to my brothers, an alien to my mother's sons."

In other words, 'I have been rejected by those closest to me (even my family) and people think I'm weird.' Why?

"For zeal for Your house has consumed me..."

'I have been rejected because my passion to be close to You, God, has consumed me.'

And then during his kingship, in his old age, I can imagine his generals, his advisors and his children gather around him one day and ask, 'David, in your whole life what is the one thing out of everything you want to be remembered for?' Remember this is now the richest, most powerful man of a generation!

You can almost hear his generals anticipating his response as they remember the glory days, 'Oh it has to be the battle when we hid in the forest and God blew the wind through the tops of the trees to tell us when to ambush the Philistines. It was glorious! (2 Samuel 5:24)'

Or you can hear his financial advisors exclaim, 'No it has to be the way you're building the city of Jerusalem as the crown of God's glory on the earth. It has to be! (2 Samuel 5:9-12)'

His children break into the conversation, 'No, no what about the time you took a sling and you were just a teenager and nobody thought anything of you. You took on a giant and won a great victory for Israel. Then you got the money and the girl! (1 Samuel 17)'

But at this point I hear David erupting, 'No, no, no, you don't understand. You're my closest friends and you don't understand me! There is only one thing I have wanted. One thing I have ever desired. There's only one thing I have always asked of the Lord,

"One thing have I asked of the LORD, that will I seek after: that I may dwell in the house of the LORD all the days

of my life, to gaze upon the beauty of the LORD *and to inquire in his temple."* (Psalm 27:4)

Delight was what motivated David's obsession and pursuit of God and His delight came from encountering who God was, the beauty of God's character and affections.

This is the cry that God saw in David's heart as he spent his days on the hills of Bethlehem with the sheep. At the core of his being, as his primary pursuit in life, David didn't want to be king, he didn't want to be rich and famous. First and foremost, he wanted his heart to be filled to overflowing with the delight that comes from encountering the beauty of God in a deeper and deeper way. He wanted to feel the affections of God toward Him and to return those affections in fiery, passionate, all-consuming love. This was the definition of his success and the foundation of his identity. This was the heart of the man who God chose FOR HIMSELF and made king of His people.

THE HEART OF THE SONG

Therefore, to discover why and how to study the Song of Songs, we need to see this book through the lens of the beauty of God. This book describes the journey God takes a man or woman on to reveal His beauty and to wholly captivate them with who He is. It describes the beauty of the way God feels toward His people all through our journey of faith. When these feelings are revealed to the human spirit they cause us to be filled with delight, fascination and burning passion for Him. There is no greater pleasure in the whole of creation. This is what we were made for! Both the beauty of God's emotions towards us and the beauty of His leadership in our lives (because of how He feels about us) are revealed through the Song of Songs.

In other words, the Song of Songs describes the 'why' behind the 'what' of the Bible. We all know the 'what' of the gospel – what Jesus did so we could be saved and the glorious rewards of this. But few people ever study or investigate the 'why' of the gospel. Why did Jesus die on the cross? What did He feel that caused Him to do what He did? What was in His heart? What is in Jesus' heart even now as He looks upon us? When we understand this, when the truth of how God feels about us hits our hearts, even a little, then we will respond with radical love in return.

Right now, God is looking for a people after His own heart. He is looking for people who know and love His character; who are students of His emotions - of the 'why' behind the 'what'. That's the kind of church Jesus is coming back for. The 'what' of the gospel is important and touches us deeply but when we begin to see the 'why' behind it then our hearts are awakened in a whole new way. We enter into a depth of relationship with our Lord that we never thought possible. Life abundant springs forth inside of us. Jesus is coming back for people who, like David, are consumed by their pursuit of His heart as a response to His emotions, thoughts and feelings (beauty) towards them. Today, the prayer rooms springing up across the earth serve as the Holy Spirit's invitation to go on this pursuit, prayer as the means and the Song of Songs as the road map of the journey God wants to take us on.

PRACTICAL 1: PURSUING THE BEAUTY OF THE LORD

Four dimensions of God's beauty:
A. God's creation (Psalm 19:1-6). This includes God's natural creation like mountains, lakes, stars, galaxies etc. but also those things you love in life, those things that touch your heart. Examples include: movies, music, experiences and/or hobbies. I guarantee that you love these things because they carry some aspect of God's beauty.

B. God's Word (Psalm 19:7-11). This includes the story God is telling through history. It is a stunning story! It is a story from which all the other stories ever told through books, plays and movies draw their inspiration. Psalm 119:103 – *How sweet are Your words to my taste, Sweeter than honey to my mouth!*

C. God's character (Song of Songs). This includes the beauty of God's feelings and thoughts towards us which we experience by revelation of the Holy Spirit (Song of Songs). It also includes His judgements which are designed to bring people to repentance and back into the experience of His love (Isaiah 26:9). Finally, it includes the journey He takes His people on to awaken their hearts to love (Psalm 19:12-14 and Song of Songs).

D. God's physical beauty (Revelation 1, 4, 5, Isaiah 6 and Ezekiel 1)

Ponder the answers to the following questions (write your answers in a journal):

1. What do you love about God? What aspects of His character do you love? Be specific. For example: *I love the way God provides. It's always unexpected. It's always out-of-left-field. It's so often at the last minute and yet so perfectly. It always brings an explosion of joy in my heart.*

2. Spend time in prayer thanking God for these things.

3. What do you love in life? What hobbies, activities, interests, experiences, movies and music do you love? Ask God to reveal Himself in these.

VALUE TWO

....

THE BEAUTY OF LONGING

Song of Songs 1:1 – The Song of Songs, which is Solomon's.

God has a secret. It's a secret written into the core of our beings from the moment we are conceived. It's a secret meant to draw us into the very heart of our maker. It's a secret crying out about who we are and what we were made for.

My favourite place in the whole world is a small national park on a rugged stretch of South Australian coast. There's a walk there, a winding path which runs down a wooded hillside and out onto yellow cliffs scoured bare by gales blasting off South Pole icebergs. The sea roars against those cliffs down below your feet. The sky is stretched, endless deep blue above. The sea glitters away as if forever to the horizon and Antarctica. When I stand on those cliffs the secret written on my heart cries out. It cries out as an ache deep inside. It's a haunting loneliness and a raging desire. It's a longing for something that, until I searched it out, I did not understand. Whether we like to admit it or not this longing is in all of us. It will not be silenced or satisfied by anything this world has to offer. We all know this if we will dial down our many thoughts and sit still long enough to let it be heard. This cry whispers to us in our joy, it calls to us through our conscience and screams in our pains (CS Lewis, *The Problem of Pain*, p.3). This longing causes us to feel perpetually that life is better on the other side of the circumstantial fence. Every now and then the stars align in our circumstances just long enough to feel as though we might have arrived at a solution to our ache. These moments always come unexpectedly. They might creep up on us while we're standing on the beach at sunset with one we love. It could happen on a holiday or at a family reunion. In those fleeting moments of love and life, it feels like we can almost touch the solution to our longing, finally obtain the life we prize. But it's always only an almost. The feeling fades so quickly, and we are left empty and the ache cries out even louder than before.

Mike Bickle describes this feeling in his book *Seven Longings of the Human Heart* (p.6). He writes: *"A longing is not even a genuine need for which we can demand satisfaction. Longing goes deeper than that. A longing is an ache of the heart. It is a cavity of the spirit crying to be filled. In its deepest sense it is neither a true verb nor a true noun, but combines the two spanning the gap between emotion and genuine need. It is an intangible feeling that ebbs and flows, yet it is a concrete reality. It cannot be reasoned with, negated or dismissed. If not attended to, it will overtake us. One way or another, whether legitimately or illegitimately, a human longing will be filled. It must be."*

I feel this longing every day of my life. Every morning I awake to the feeling deep down in my chest that there must be something more to life than what I'm experiencing. Trying to live in the moment is difficult because I find myself striving to get to something or somewhere which is strangely elusive. It doesn't matter how enjoyable life is, something always feels missing. In response, I try to numb the longing by distracting myself with other things - relationships, activities, possessions. Yet the ache won't leave me.

I also mistake the deeper longing in my heart as a longing for something I can see with my eyes in the natural. So I go out and work to obtain the thing I believe will satisfy me. Then when I finally obtain the object of my desire I find my heart aches just the same, perhaps more.

OUR HEAVENLY HOME

The secret of longing God has written on our hearts is the truth we are made to be with Him forever. This truth "...*will not be reasoned with, negated or dismissed.*" David's son, Solomon, knew of this truth when he wrote in Ecclesiastes 3:11, "...*He has put eternity into man's heart...*" King Solomon came to understand that this ache we all feel is a longing for a happy ending, a secure future and blissful union with our maker. In the difference our hearts perceive between the broken world around us and the eternity written on our hearts comes longing (John Eldredge, *The Journey of Desire*, 2000). For example, a mother and father divorce and in the heart of their little son arises a longing for family which will not be silenced. He knows something is not right because it is written on his heart (and ours) that we are made to live in family, with God in perfection, forever. We are made to sit with Jesus on His throne, to judge angels and rule the created universe (Revelation 3:21; 1 Corinthians 6:3; Revelation 5:10). We are made to feel God's delight and pleasure over us and to know Him and be perfectly known (1 Corinthians 13:12). Therefore, in the difference between the reality of the world and this truth, longing is aroused. Thankfully, this also speaks of the truth that there is a day coming when our longing will be fulfilled.

In John 14, Jesus promises to take us to a place where our deepest longing would be satisfied.

"Let not your hearts be troubled. Believe in God; believe also in me. In my Father's house are many rooms. If it were not so, would I have told you that I go to prepare a place for you? And if I go and prepare a place for you, I will come again and will take you to myself, that where I am you may be also." (John 14:1-3).

In the book of Revelation, the apostle John saw visions of these mansions in a city of gold and called by God the New Jerusalem (Revelation 21, 22). The New Jerusalem is where we will live with God for eternity. It is our home. It is where we truly belong. This is what the ache in our hearts is telling us.

WHY LONGING?

Let us go one level deeper. Why has God put this longing in our hearts? Why has God written this deep ache into the core of our being? It is a truth hard to fully grasp in its depth and implications. The answer in short: God wrote this longing into us because He longs for us. We have longing in our hearts because God has longing in His. The singer-songwriter Plumb (*God-Shaped Hole*, 1999), sings, *"There's a God-shaped hole in all of us and the restless soul is searching."* This is our longing. But have you ever realised God has allowed there to be a you-shaped hole in His heart? You have a God-shaped hole in your heart because He has a You-shaped hole in His. You were made to fill this hole in a way nobody else ever can. Nobody else can move God's heart in the way you can (Song of Songs 6:9).

And because of this truth, each of us, individually, can call ourselves God's favourite one. Can you believe this? There is no one else like YOU. You are His favourite one!

Our longings are but small reflections of the great longing in His heart. He has written six thousand years of history as the story of His furious longing for people. Consider this:

- In the Garden of Eden, God walked with Adam and Eve in the cool of the evening.
- When this communion was broken, God set in motion His plan to bring restoration of relationship through Jesus (Genesis 3:15).

The Song Jesus Sings

- When God brought the Jewish people out of captivity in Egypt, He took Moses up the mountain and commanded him to build a tabernacle that He might dwell amongst His people once again (Exodus 19:5, 6).
- When God brought the Israelites out of exile in Babylon the first thing He commanded them was to rebuild the temple that He might dwell again with them. As the years passed and the people gained prosperity for themselves while the temple remained unbuilt, God rebuked them through the prophet Haggai (1:4), *"Is it time for you yourselves to dwell in your paneled houses, while this house lies in ruins?"*
- When the prophet Isaiah speaks of the coming messiah He proclaims Him as Immanuel, God with us. (Isaiah 7:14; Matthew 1:23)
- And in John 17:24, as Jesus is about to go to the cross He looks heavenward and cries out: *"Father, I desire that they also whom You have given Me may be with Me where I am..."*

Again and again, obvious in every book of the Bible, the desire of God is this: I want to dwell with my people!

Can you imagine it, have you perceived it? The God of the universe who sits on the throne of heaven, ruling forever and ever desires to be with you. All of heaven, the four living creatures, the 24 elders and thousands upon thousands of angels cry out, day and night, *"Holy, holy, holy,"* and yet the God who deserves and receives all of this unceasing worship is lovesick for your heart to be turned toward His (Revelation 4:8). This is not some small desire in a corner of God's great heart crowded out by a myriad of other thoughts and pressing business. This is what is on His mind day and night! *"How precious to me are your thoughts, O God! How vast is the sum of them! If I would count them, they are more than the sand..."* (Psalm 139:17, 18) What does God do day and night on His throne? He thinks about YOU!

Jesus went to the cross because of His longing for you. You are the joy that was set before Him (Hebrews 12:2) His is the desire of a bridegroom who longs for the day of His wedding. Though He despised the shame of death His love and longing overruled His natural human tendency toward self-preservation (Hebrews 12:2). This is a love and longing so overwhelming our weak human frames can barely begin to comprehend it. When this truth touches our hearts, it has the power to totally transform the way we live. It causes our hearts to come alive in a way we never thought possible.

JESUS, THE WORD OF GOD

As I ponder and meditate and read about Jesus and the longing of His heart throughout the Bible I imagine right now He is walking on the golden streets of our heavenly home. He is checking the houses, watching the river which flows through the city and dreaming of the day when we will be with Him. Hebrews 7:25 describes how Jesus always lives to intercede for us at the right hand of the Father. His is a life of longing and His intercession goes something like this: *"Father, I DESIRE!"*

I also believe Jesus is singing. In our human experience we know singing always comes as the overflow of a heart of longing, passion and desire. It's the overflow of a person in love. I believe it is the same with Jesus. Right now, He is singing in heaven and His singing has deep significance for what the Holy Spirit is doing across the earth today.

Before the dawn of time, the Father, Son and Holy Spirit, the great unfathomable, uncreated, unending God had a meeting. The Father had a plan and this plan was to write a story, a sweeping epic spread across time and space, the story from which all other stories are inspired. It was a story designed to express and show for all to see the greatness of God and the majesty of His heart which is love. This story was to be one great, 'THIS IS WHO I AM' statement. The main character of the story, the hero of the story, was to be Jesus.

In this conference the Father shared His plan with the Son and the Spirit. You can find a brief description of it in Revelation 1:1 –

"The Revelation of Jesus Christ, which God gave Him to show His servants..."

In other words, God the Father, gave Jesus Christ (Him) the storyline to reveal to His people. During this meeting, filled with humility, love and passion, the Son agreed with every detail.

"For all the promises of God find their Yes in Him....." (2 Corinthians 1:20)

This verse is a very clinical way of describing the 'yes' of Jesus to the plan of the Father. I think His 'yes' was more like the roar of a mighty lion or a terrible wave in the midst of a storm. The whole of heaven shook at the explosion of passion and agreement from His heart. In full agreement the Son, the

Word of God, spoke the beginning of the plan, the beginning of creation saying,

"*Let there be light*" (Genesis 1:3) and the Spirit, "*...hovering over the face of the waters...*" (Genesis 1:2) in worked to bring the will of the Father and Word of the Son into being.

This was the order of the trinity then and this is the order of the trinity now. The Father has the plan, the Son puts words to the plan and the Spirit works to bring it to being.

THE SONG OF ALL SONGS

This same order describes how the Bible came into being. 2 Timothy 3:16 says, "*All scripture is breathed out by God...*"

The Father revealed His will to the Son, the Son spoke this will and the Holy Spirit moved on the hearts of people to write, to copy, to protect and to translate those Words throughout all the turbulent seasons of human history.

King David's son Solomon was king in Israel right after David and, in an even greater measure than his father, was a man of wisdom, songs and poetry. Across his lifetime, he wrote 3000 proverbs and 1005 songs (1 Kings 4:32). Yet while many of his proverbs are now scripture, only one of his songs ever made it into the Bible. The Song of Songs is a song sung by Solomon to his bride, the Shulamite (a woman of Shunem/Shulam). It is filled with what can be interpreted as sexual symbolism describing the ecstasy of married love. Yet if Jesus truly is the Word of God then it must be asked whether the Song of Songs was originally Solomon's at all? Could it be this Song was originally sung by Jesus in the streets of the Holy City as He longed for the day of His wedding? Time and again through the Bible, Jesus is described as a Bridegroom returning to His people, His bride, His church. Could it be this is the Song sung by Jesus over His people throughout human history and the Holy Spirit moved on Solomon's heart to write it down and the hearts of God-fearing men and women to include it in scripture? Could it be Jesus is again singing this song in the streets of heaven and so the Holy Spirit is moving on the hearts of God's people to highlight it and the story it describes in our time?

Truly we live in a glorious time of history. I believe that right now King Jesus is standing in heaven and singing the Song of Solomon over us. As He sings the Holy Spirit is moving across the earth to draw people into the journey outlined in the book, into the journey that will prepare the Church as the

The Song Jesus Sings

bride Jesus longs for, as a bride worthy of Him. As a bride with a passion similar in intensity to His own.

Jesus loves and longs for us with ALL of His heart. He desires a bride who loves and longs for Him with ALL of her heart. His strategy for raising up a bride like this is to awaken longing in our hearts for Him by allowing us to feel the longing for us that is in His.

Zephaniah 3:17 – *The LORD your God is in your midst, a mighty one who will save;*
he will rejoice over you with gladness; he will quiet you by his love; he will exult over you with loud singing.

PRACTICAL 2: AWAKENING LONGING

Right now, God is inviting His people to awaken to longing. Firstly, He is inviting us to become aware of the lesser longings of our hearts. There are three things we can do with our longings. We all have a tendency to do the first two and skip the third. 1) We can try to satisfy our longings ourselves with the things of the world. 2) We can try to ignore them and push them down into our subconscious. 3) We can turn them into prayer and pursuit of God.

Here's a thought. Could it be when longing arises in our hearts, when you have a craving for vanilla Coke at 11pm on a Saturday night, that God is actually knocking on the door of your heart and desiring to commune with you in that moment?

When we take option three, God begins to make us aware of our eternal longing for Him. Next, He takes us on the journey of satisfying our hearts by revealing the longing He has for us. There is nothing more satisfying in our lives than God revealing God to the human spirit. In the place of bringing our longings into the place of prayer and beginning to experience the furious longing of His heart for us, our hearts come fully alive in burning passion for Him.

The Song Jesus Sings

Answer these questions in your journal
1. What are the longings of your heart?

2. What do you do with the longings of your heart?

3. Read through 1 Samuel 1-3. This is the story of God using the longing of a woman named Hannah to restore the nation of Israel. Can you see how Hannah's longing works to bring God's redemptive plan for Israel about? Study this passage closely. Ask the Lord to reveal truth to you in these chapters.

4. Now bring the lesser longings of your heart to God in prayer. Wait to see what He will say about them. Begin a journey of asking the Lord about the lesser longings of your heart: job, marriage, family, retirement, etc.

VALUE THREE

....

THE DIVINE KISS

Song of Songs 1:2 – Let him kiss me with the kisses of his mouth; for your love is better than wine.

The cold of morning crept in under the front door and breathed across the clean concrete floor as the man picked up his little, curly haired son and wrapped him, head to toe, in the blue and white tallis, a Jewish prayer shawl. The man carried his son then, out the door and down the hill to the school. It was his son's first day of school, a significant day in Jewish culture. The little boy was placed on the knee of the Rabbi and a new writing slate was brought inscribed with the 10 commandments of Moses. A drop of honey was placed next to each letter of the alphabet written on the slate. The Rabbi began to read one letter at a time and the boy repeated it and licked the honey and the Rabbi said, *"How sweet are Your words to my taste, sweeter than honey to my mouth!"* (Psalm 119:103) This was the tradition practiced for hundreds of years as Jewish children were taught the Word of God (*A child's entry into cheder*, Eli Touger, 2016).

KNOWING THE WORD

Brought up in the Jewish tradition described above many of the men and women of the Bible experienced the sweetness of God's Word. Ezekiel and John the apostle are excellent examples. They consumed the Word of God and found it as sweet as honey.

"And he said to me, "Son of man, eat whatever you find here. Eat this scroll, and go, speak to the house of Israel." 2 So I opened my mouth, and he gave me this scroll to eat. 3 And he said to me, "Son of man, feed your belly with this scroll that I give you and fill your stomach with it." Then I ate it, and it was in my mouth as sweet as honey." – (Ezekiel 3:1-3)

"And I took the little scroll from the hand of the angel and ate it. It was sweet as honey in my mouth, but when I had eaten it my stomach was made bitter." – (Revelation 10:10)

The Song Jesus Sings

The Word of God is still the same today. It is still the primary vehicle the Holy Spirit uses to reveal the beauty and longing of Jesus to the hearts of God's people. It is the written revelation of who He is and it's not just 'a telling' of Him but a revealing, a showing of His character and nature through story.

In writing school, we were taught again and again to show rather than tell in our creative pieces. We were taught we needed to show who our characters were - not just tell our readers about them. An example of this is shown below.

Character description: Danny was angry.

Question: How did Danny feel?

Answer: Danny felt angry.

This is telling.

Now to show:

Character description: Danny kicked and screamed and threw the book across the room.

Question: How did Danny feel?

Answer: Danny felt angry.

In both examples, it's the same character feeling the same emotion, yet it is an entirely different way to discover a person. It is actually the way we develop friendships with one another. We learn about each other and come to trust by observing the consistency of how another person acts through all the events of life. A person can tell us about themselves, 'Oh, I'm a happy person.' But if they never behave happy, we won't believe what they've told us. The truth of action we see with our own eyes is far more powerful to us than words. In our time God is once again calling His Church to return to the ancient path, the old way of finding delight in the discovery of God through the story of His Word.

THE DIVINE KISS

Going a level deeper, there is more to finding delight and pleasure in the Bible than only knowing God's story in an intellectual way. There is also a supernatural element to the delight God has for us in His Word. This is spoken of in Song of Songs 1:2.

Observe the verse. There's something strange about it. Instead of the bride saying to Jesus, "Would you kiss me?" she says, "Let him kiss me." It appears there is some third party to whom she's talking and asking. In fact, she is speaking to the Father. She is crying out to the Father to allow His Son, Jesus, to kiss her.

When you or I kiss, it is a passionate exchange of affection from one mouth to another, from one heart to another. It's an intimate connection that runs far deeper than lips touching. It's an exchange which cannot but move your heart.

The bride asks the Father to let the Son kiss her with the kisses of His mouth. What comes from the mouth of Jesus? What is Jesus called in John 1:1? He is the Word of God. Another way to write this verse then would be: *Let Him kiss me with the kisses of His Word.*

In this verse the bride is crying out for Father God to release the Holy Spirit to touch her heart with the Words of Jesus. She is crying out for her heart to connect with the heart of her Bridegroom by the power of the Holy Spirit so that she might know Him and draw close to Him.

The Holy Spirit which dwells inside of a born-again believer is the same Holy Spirit who was present at the creation of the world; the same Holy Spirit who saw David write Psalm 27:4; the same Holy Spirit who witnessed Jesus die on the cross;

the same Holy Spirit who still today searches the deep things of God in order to make them known to us (1 Corinthians 2:10). There are things about God revealed through the Word which we could never find out by an intellectual knowledge of the Bible alone. It is the Holy Spirit who must reveal them to us. Yes, an intellectual knowledge by reading and study is where we need to start... but there is more! In the same way it is possible to know a lot of information about a person without really knowing the person themselves, it is possible to know about God through His Word without really knowing God Himself. Truly knowing a person and truly knowing God involves a connection of hearts.

Here's another analogy. An intellectual knowledge of the Word to our hearts is like the sticks of a bonfire. The sticks are necessary for a bonfire, but they are not a bonfire themselves. The sticks of intellectual knowledge in our hearts need the spark of the Holy Spirit before they come alive and bring our relationship with God to life. When the spark of the Holy Spirit comes, the Word of God becomes a passionate exchange between our heart and Jesus' heart. We can actually begin to experience Jesus' emotions (His longing and His affections) toward us. The Word is no longer dry then. This is where the Word truly becomes sweeter than honey.

When the Holy Spirit does what the Holy Spirit loves to do and touches our hearts with God's Word, then we catch an experience of the beauty of Jesus' emotions. As this happens our hearts become raging bonfires of passion for Jesus in response. As Mike Bickle says, *"If you want to get passion for Jesus, study Jesus' passion for you."* (*Live Holy: Living fascinated in the pleasure of Loving God*, 2010) Ask the Holy Spirit to come and let you actually experience His passion for you. If you want to get a burning heart, fill your mind and heart with the truth of God's Word and pray the prayer the bride in Song of Songs prays, *"Let Him kiss me with the kisses of his mouth!"* There is no other experience sweeter to the human heart in the whole created order than the divine kiss of His Word!

CREATED TO ENJOY GOD

Jonathan Edwards, the great puritan revivalist, preacher and theologian of the 1700s wrote:"...God glorifies himself towards the creatures [us] also [in] two ways: (1) by appearing to them, being manifested to their understanding; (2) in communicating himself to their hearts, and in their rejoicing and delighting in, and enjoying the manifestations which he makes of himself. . . . God is glorified not only by his glory's being seen, but by its being rejoiced in. . . ." (Edwards, The "Miscellanies," The Works of Jonathan Edwards, vol. 13, [Yale University Press, 1994], p. 495)

In modern English Jonathan Edwards is saying: we are meant to not only know and understand God intellectually but to find delight and joy through our understanding. This delight is not some ethereal feeling divorced from knowledge and understanding. It is not a giddy rolling on the floor or jumping up and down because we feel something, though we will feel something. It is a deep and profound joy flowing out of deep knowledge and understanding because we have now added experience to what was previously theory. It is not theory anymore, it is truth, experiential knowing. It is not someone else's story anymore, it's our story.

To have experience and emotion without knowledge is to not really know God at all. But to know about God intellectually alone is but half the Christian experience. God's Word is meant to move our hearts to delight. Such delight will bring forth passionate love in our hearts for Him. This is what we were made for. It is our inheritance (2 Corinthians 11:2). Let us not settle for anything less!

The Song Jesus Sings

A LOVE BETTER THAN WINE

The bride goes on in verse 2 to describe the experience explained above, the effect of the kiss of Jesus' Word, *"for your love is better than wine."* In verse two she is saying, 'I'm crying out for the kiss of Jesus' Word because the beauty of His affections revealed to my heart is better than anything this world has to offer.'

When we experience the emotions of Jesus' heart through the Word and the Spirit it is an experience so overwhelming, remarkable and perfectly suited to the human heart that the most pleasurable, thrilling things this world has to offer will seem worthless in comparison. They will seem broken and useless. Surely, having experience of such love will sustain us even through trial and difficulty.

King David knew this truth when He wrote in Psalm 63:3 – *"Because your steadfast love is better than life, my lips will praise you."* Paul also knew it when He wrote in Philippians 3:8 –

"Indeed, I count everything as loss because of the surpassing worth of knowing Christ Jesus my Lord. For his sake I have suffered the loss of all things and count them as rubbish, in order that I may gain Christ..."

We were made to be caught up in the affections of Jesus to where nothing else will satisfy no matter how hard we try to convince ourselves.

Writing these sentences tears are pooling in my eyes as I remember a time when there was nothing I wanted to do more than sit in His sweet presence and encounter the beauty of His emotions toward me. He was truly my drug and my addiction.

I remember one year in my early twenties how my friends and I would gather together on Friday and Saturday nights and wonder what we should do. Someone would say, "Let's pray," so we would. Someone would get out a guitar and we'd worship too. The Holy Spirit would show up, tears would flow and joy would overtake us as Jesus revealed His heart for us. Then God would give us pictures of people lost and broken in the pubs and clubs on those Friday and Saturday nights and we would go out to share this love that is better than life. That year was the best year of my life. That was the year I became an addict – an addict to encountering God and knowing Him more deeply.

Encountering God's affections changed me. Even the legitimate pleasures of this world, the things I used to enjoy so much before I really encountered God (like playing soccer and camping and hiking) have dulled in comparison to the indescribable ecstasy of having Jesus kiss me with His Word. This is what it means, *"his love is better than wine."* Wine represents the pleasures of this world. Many of them are legitimate pleasures but none of them compare to the love of God which transcends understanding and description.

WHAT IS GOD INVITING US TO?

Many people believe they've encountered God and likely they have in part. But I can tell you from experience and from the Bible that when we truly encounter God the response is a raging passion for Jesus and complimentary desire to give up everything as a response and in the pursuit of more of Him. We may not yet have the strength to fully give up everything, but it will become the longing of our heart to lavish our lives upon Jesus. Just look at the disciples. When Peter encounters Jesus as the promised Messiah, he lays down his nets, his livelihood, his future and follows (Luke 5). When Mary of Bethany understands Jesus as the Son of God she takes a jar of pure nard, her entire inheritance, and pours it out, wasting it as act of worship upon Him (Matthew 26). The response to having our hearts kissed by Jesus is always extravagant worship and devotion.

Sadly, for the most part in our logic driven Western society, we have lost this "experiential" understanding of God's Word. Most of our Western Christian culture revolves around the premise that Christianity involves 'knowing the right thing' and 'doing the right thing.' Now don't get me wrong, knowing the right thing and doing the right thing are vitally important. In John 14:15 Jesus defines love for Him as obedience. But what should our primary motivation for obedience be? 1 John 4:10 says, *"In this is love, not that we have loved God but that he loved us and sent his Son..."* In other words, only by an experiential understanding of God's love can we love God in return. It is impossible for us to truly love God unless we have first experienced His love for us. First and foremost, our love for God expressed through obedience is meant to be a response, a reflex, an overflow of our experience of His affection toward us. This is what the bride in the Song of Songs knows. This is what she is asking for. She knows her experience of God's love is sweeter than the taste of honey, more delightful than a kiss, and will lead her to extravagant obedience and devotion. She cries out: *"Let him kiss me with the kisses of his mouth..."* 'Let Your Son touch my heart with His Word of love which is like a passionate kiss!'

The Song Jesus Sings

This second verse of the Song of Songs is the beginning of the bride's journey into deep intimacy. This verse encapsulates what God is calling His people to across the earth. God is inviting us to stop business as usual, to let the things of this world be put in their proper place, to come and sit at His feet, to hear His voice and encounter His longing and affection toward us. The way we do this is to open our dusty, forgotten Bibles and begin to read, pray and be still long enough for His fiery love to reveal the beautiful longing and affection of His heart to our own.

We were made for more than dutiful obedience and dry knowledge. We were made for passionate pursuit and all-consuming delight in God and His Word.

PRACTICAL 3: FINDING DELIGHT IN GOD'S WORD - PART 1

A. Firstly, when we read, we need to go wide by reading the whole Bible from beginning to end. This is important because **the Bible interprets the Bible**. We need to know what is in it and how the different parts relate to each other. For example, we can learn a lot by comparing Isaiah 6 and Revelation 4 and 5. As we start to see connections throughout the Bible, the story of God will begin to come alive in our minds. It really will!

B. Secondly, when we read it is **important to also go deep**. We need to study and meditate and memorise single verses and chapters and books of the Bible until they seep into our subconscious, we digest them and begin to live and breathe them.

C. Finally, **we need to turn the Word into prayer**. The Hebrew word for 'meditate' [hâgâh] means 'to utter or vocalize'. We need to turn the passages we love and have studied deeply into prayers back to God. It's through prayer that God softens our hearts and kisses them by the Holy Spirit.

Practical exercises
1. Set a goal to read a certain number of Bible chapters every day. While I was serving full-time in the House of Prayer I read 10 chapters a day. However, now I am working I don't have the time or energy to read this much and only read 1-2 chapters a day. I still have a goal though.

   Set a goal which is manageable and sustainable. Start at Genesis and read to Revelation. As you read, if there are times you find your mind wandering, **don't** go back and reread the bits you didn't take in. Just keep going. If you go back, you'll quickly become discouraged. As you read look for connections between the different passages and books.

2. One of the most enjoyable ways to go deep in passages of scripture is to find an aspect of the story in them which moves you. To do this start with the stories in the gospels. Choose a story you really like and then in your imagination or on paper (by writing or

drawing) turn this story into a little movie script. This involves the following steps:

a) You need to know the passage really well so read it out loud to yourself a few times.
b) Ask questions about things which don't make sense in the passage.
c) Write them down and ask the Holy Spirit to reveal the answers to you (it may take time for the Holy Spirit to respond so be patient).

For example: John 9 - **Question:** Why is the blind man begging if he has parents? **Answer the Holy Spirit gave me:** The parents were too poor to look after the son anymore and so he had to go and beg for a living. **Can you see how this begins to open up a whole storyline? Now you begin to wonder, so why were the parents so poor?**
Now try to visualise the whole story in your imagination or write it on paper.

3. There are two main kinds of passages in the Bible: promises to believe and exhortations to obey. For example:

A Biblical promise: John 15:9a – *As the Father has loved me, so have I loved you...*
A Biblical exhortation: John 15:9b – *...abide in my love.*

Start by focusing on God's promises. Thank God for them and ask Him to help you experience the power of them in your life. For example, with John 15:9a pray: 'Jesus, I thank You that You love me in the same way that the Father loves You. That You love me with the same intensity of love that the Father loves You. Father help me to experience more of Your love.'

We can know about God's promises without ever really experiencing them. Ask Him for an event to take place in your life which will allow you to experience a particular promise to the same degree of reality to which you experience the affection of a loved one through a kiss or hug. This is available! God wants to bring the promises of His Word alive to this extent in our lives!

VALUE FOUR

....

WEAK YET LOVELY TO GOD

Song of Songs 1:5 – I am very dark, but lovely, O daughters of Jerusalem, like the tents of Kedar, like the curtains of Solomon.

In the previous chapter I described the power of the Word to give us the experience of Jesus' emotions toward us. One of those emotions is His longing for us (explored in Value 2). Another is the profound truth of God calling us lovely, even in the midst of our weakness; of God continuing to enjoy us even in our immaturity and despite our tendency to fail. The practical implications of this truth to our lives are immense. When the truth of how God feels about us even in our weakness and failure touches our hearts it will revolutionize our lives.

NATURAL IDENTITY VS SPIRITUAL IDENTITY

What motivates you? What is it, deep down, which causes joy to spring forth in your heart? Whether we realise it or not, the truth is that many of us are primarily motivated by how we compare to others. We draw our sense of success and value from how we compare to those around us. Truth be told, most of us find our primary source of value in how much money we have, how popular we are, how much impact we have, what we own, what we're good at, how we dress and whether we have a good job.

Deep down, all of us believe on some level that our value is based on how we measure up to others. When we compare well we are happy because we feel valuable and successful and when we compare poorly we are miserable because we feel worthless and unsuccessful.

And how would we not believe this? It is the way our world operates. It is the value system we have lived under all our lives. It is naturally how we define ourselves. The truth is, nobody alive has enough money, talent, possessions, friends or status to feel good about themselves even some of the time. Living from this identity causes us to behave as if we are fighting for scraps of love on the floor when, as the beloved of God, an unending banquet of love and value is freely offered to us. We are doomed to feel like failures when we live with our natural identities as our primary source of identity.

Yet when Jesus hung on the cross, freed His lungs one last time and yelled *"It is finished!"* in triumph across the stillness of ancient Jerusalem (John 19:30), he made a way for us to live from a new source of life. Jesus called it a spring of living water in John 4. It is the place of knowing how God feels and how God defines us. This is a deeper truth of the gospel so many of us have missed.

WEAK AM I YET LOVELY

To explore this deeper we need to go back to Song of Songs 1. Back in verse 2, we saw how the bride started her journey by crying out for Jesus to touch her heart with the kiss of His Word. Now we skip forward to verse 4.

Verse 4 has four sections. While it is only about 40 words in length (dependant on the exact translation you're reading), it captures a pitfall in the Christian journey with which many of us are familiar: burnout and extreme exhaustion in ministry.

Song of Songs 1:4
   Section 1 - THE SHULAMITE
   Draw me after you; let us run (together).

   Section 2 - THE SHULAMITE
   The king has brought me into his chambers.

   Section 3 - THE DAUGHTERS OF JERUSALEM
   We will exult and rejoice in you;
      we will extol your love more than wine;

   Section 4 - THE SHULAMITE
   rightly do they love you.

The first section of verse 4 finds the bride crying out for the Bridegroom to take her away with Him. *"Draw me after you; let us run* (together)" she cries. It is an extension of verse 2 where she asked for the kisses of His Word. It proclaims the desire of her heart and the vision of her life to be drawn into intimacy with the Bridegroom and into ministry alongside Him.

In the next sentence, (section 2 of verse 4) the Bride declares, *"The king has brought me into his chambers."* The chamber of the king represents the place of deep intimacy and encounter with Jesus. It is the place where He kisses us with the kisses of His mouth (Word) and reveals the affections and longing of His heart toward us. For any king it would only have been his most intimate friends, relatives, wife and children who were ever allowed to enter his personal chambers. This phrase shows how Jesus has answered the Bride's prayers and drawn her into the place of deep intimacy by the kiss of His Word. The Hebrew phrasing literally means: a chamber inside a chamber. It reminds us of the Holy of Holies in the tabernacle of Moses and the temple of Solomon. It is the most intimate place of encounter with the living, Holy God. It is a place which, for the Jewish people, could only be entered by the High Priest once a year. However, now, because of the blood of our desiring King, all we must do is cry out: *Let him kiss me with the kisses of his mouth!*

The third section of verse 4 introduces us to the third character in the Song of Songs: the Daughters of Jerusalem. The Daughters of Jerusalem represent those close friends of the bride who are:

1) observing the life of the bride;
2) remembering the life of the bride and commenting on it; as well as
3) longing to go on the same journey.

In this reading of the Song, there is a significant time gap (of months, perhaps years) between sections 2 and 3 of verse 4 (remember, we are exploring the Song of Songs as a journey with Jesus across a lifetime). Here in this third section the Daughters of Jerusalem are trying to remind the bride (who has now fallen into compromise) of her previous experience in the King's chamber.

"We will exult and rejoice in you; (the bride), *we will extol your* (the Bridegroom's) *love more than wine* (the things of this world)."

In essence they are saying, 'Oh we remember how you cried out for the kiss of Jesus' Word and testified that His love is better than the things of this world. We remember how you were so alive in that past season!'

Finally, the fourth section of verse 4 is a winsome cry emanating from the bride as she remembers her past experience in the King's chamber, a time she has not experienced for a long time now. *"Rightly do they love you,"* she cries. Here the bride is saying, 'Oh now I remember! I had forgotten but now I remember again. I remember the time when I experienced Your love for me, Jesus. The Daughters of Jerusalem are so right to celebrate Your love!'

What took place in the space of one phrase between the chamber of the King and the winsome remembering of this place again? If we skip down to verse 6 the answer becomes clear. Here the bride laments: *Do not look upon me, because I am dark.*

She is admitting she has sinned and fallen away from the intimacy she once experienced. Why? *"because the sun has looked upon me,"* (Song of Songs 1:6) she explains. The sun represents the cruelty and harshness of the world and its ways which have no regard for those with tender hearts (see Mark 4:6 and Note 3). And now the reason for the bride's slip into sin: *My mother's sons were angry with me; They made me the keeper of the vineyards, but my own vineyard I have not kept!* The mother here represents the institutional church and the mother's sons are brothers (and sisters) in the church (see Galatians 4:26-28). Vineyards represent the hearts of believers, the deep intimate place from which the source of our emotional and spiritual energy flows (Proverbs 4:23; John 15).

What do so many of us do when we really encounter Jesus for the first time? We rush into ministry. What do many church leaders do when they find someone "on fire" for Jesus? They push them into ministry. How do many people in the church (the mother's sons) feel when someone who is passionately in love with God tells them there is more to their Christian walk than what they are experiencing? They are angry and offended and write them off as immature and going through "a stage."

This is the complex, distressing reality verse 6 describes. This is what took place between sections 2 and 3 of this verse. This is the place the bride now finds herself. In response to encountering Jesus' love in the chamber of the King, the bride is pushed into ministry and into caring for the hearts of others. She becomes so busy in her ministry she neglects her own vineyard, her own heart connection with Jesus, her own secret place (Matthew 6:6).

When we truly encounter Jesus for the first time our initial reaction is usually to rush out to tell others. With so much good intention and passion bursting from our hearts, we rush into ministry to share with others this love that is better than the things of the world (wine). There we are met with anger and condemnation and accusation that we are arrogant, proud and acting spiritually superior. In our busyness and desire to share God's love we desert the secret place of communion with Christ (e.g. the King's chamber (Matthew 6:6)). This is the very place where our heart and soul have come alive as we've encountered the beauty of Jesus' affections toward us. In our immature zeal we leave the very place our spiritual and emotional life comes from.

After some months or years, we find ourselves spiritually and emotionally burnt out. Then with empty, tired hearts old addictions and habits rear their heads again and we find ourselves returning to the places where we used to find comfort. Finally, we descend into despair and condemnation. Why couldn't we cope? Why couldn't we manage? Did we misunderstand the heart of Jesus for others? Was that encounter we had in the previous season even real? These are the cries which so naturally issue forth from our hearts. It is the natural response of immature love. Yet our King knows our weakness and stands ready to answer. King Jesus has a plan to bring us to a place where we won't burn out. He remembers the cry of the bride's heart at the beginning of verse 4 to *"run together"* in ministry. King Jesus also knows His love, which we did encounter previously, is wide enough and long enough and deep enough and high enough to see us through the journey. Verse 5 holds the answers to our questioning hearts in the midst of failure.

In verse 5, the bride, echoes forth the stunning revelation of how Jesus defines her. She says, *I am very dark, but lovely*. In other words: 'though I have sinned, I know He still sees me as beautiful.' *Like the tents of Kedar, like the curtains of Solomon*. 'Black like the tents of the inhabitants of Arabia (Kedar) is my sin yet You, my King, still see me as beautiful like the curtains hanging in Solomon's temple.' Here the bride speaks forth the stunning revelation that Jesus defines us by what we shall be and long to be rather than our present inability to live up to that high vision. Jesus defines us by the cry in our hearts to love Him even though our love is weak. This verse encapsulates the deeper truth of the gospel, easily missed, and yet so dynamic in drawing the human spirit into the fullness of life that Jesus has for us. The profound truth about how God evaluates us is the spiritual identity that God offers.

I'M THE ONE JESUS LOVES

Here's another example. In Luke 9:46-48, the apostle John is on the ministry road with Jesus and the other disciples. I can imagine Jesus walked ahead of the group to have a private conversation with Peter or one of the others. The other 11 disciples walked behind and talked as young men do. In time, a dispute arose amongst them as to which was to be the greatest. In other words, one of the boys (we find out in Mark 9 it was John who led the discussion) decided he was no longer content with being one of the top 12 men in history. He wanted to be above the other eleven. It quickly became apparent he was not the first to have this thought. They'd all been comparing themselves to each other for a while now and secretly wanting to be the greatest.

An onlooker could have pointed out they were already destined to be defined as some of the most successful men in history. They were already destined to be recorded in the Word of God, have their names written on the foundations of the New Jerusalem and chosen to be the first leaders of a movement which would transform the world. Yet the disciples weren't content with this. Each of them wanted to be above the other eleven. The point here is they were seriously connected to what they looked like to others. They were still living from the place of their natural identity. Jesus rebukes them in verse 48:

"Whoever receives this child in my name receives me, and whoever receives me receives him who sent me. For he who is least among you all is the one who is great."

You'd think this rebuke would make John think a little harder about his ambition and comparative spirit. Yet in verse 49 we find John answering the rebuke in a surprising fashion. He's just been scolded for a lack of humility and so he says to Jesus,

"*Master, we saw someone casting out demons in your name, and we tried to stop him, because he does not follow with us.*"

In other words, he says, 'We found these other people who were casting out demons in your name. And they were really anointed by the Holy Spirit and the demons really came out. So we told them to stop because we don't want anyone outside our little group having any power. We want to be the main people.' Again, someone on the outside might say, 'John that's not a very good response to the rebuke you just received.' Jesus rebukes him again:

"*But Jesus said to him, "Do not stop him, for the one who is not against you is for you.""* (verse 50).

Finally, through verses 53 – 56 John pipes up once more. Now they've just been refused entry into a Samaritan village and when James and John see this they come to Jesus with indignation and say:

"*Lord, do you want us to tell fire to come down from heaven and consume them?*"

In other words: 'they didn't want us to have an outreach in their town. I mean we're the main guys. This is an outrage! Can we command fire to fall from heaven and just destroy the whole town?' For the third time in ten verses, Jesus rebukes John (see Luke 9:55, 56 – NKJV).

The Song Jesus Sings

The point of these three experiences is that John was intimately connected with how he compared to others. He was motivated by whether he was more important, more influential and more famous than anyone else. He also got himself in trouble many times. By the standards most of us hold ourselves to, we would have to conclude he was selfish, arrogant, prideful and self-righteous. Yet, as he continued to journey with Jesus through the years, something changed in him. Throughout the gospel of John, though he is the author, John never refers to himself by name. Instead in the last few chapters of the book we see his inner transformation. Between chapters 13 (the last supper) and the end of the gospel, John refers to himself as *"the disciple whom Jesus loves."*

In his journey, John had a revelation. He failed many times. He was one of the eleven in the garden who fled when Jesus was arrested, abandoning his Lord and master. Yet he came to a place where he could say, 'I am not defined by my weakness and failure. I am not defined by what other people think of me or by how I compare to others. I know I was arrogant and prideful in wanting to be the greatest. I know I wanted to be the main guy and to even see other people die to prove my superiority. I know I abandoned Jesus in His hour of greatest need. I know I am still full of weakness in how I love God.

But this is not what defines me. At the core of my being this is who I am: I'm the one Jesus loves! I am the one that Jesus likes. I am the one that Jesus enjoys.' This man, who was so immature and failed so often and struggled so greatly, came to realise that he knew that he knew that he knew: "he was the disciple Jesus loved!"

Jesus imparted this same identity to the apostle Peter. You can find the story in John 21. Peter is the one specifically highlighted in scripture as a denier of Jesus. He didn't only flee the soldiers in the garden. His failure was much deeper by human standards. He said with his own mouth, not once, not twice but three times: *"I do not know the man!"* (Matthew 26:72) Jesus comes to Peter by the Sea of Galilee (John 21). Now remember, Jesus called Peter as a disciple way back in Luke 5 when He said, standing on the shore of the Sea of Galilee, *"Put out into the deep and let down your nets for a catch."* (v.4) Though Peter had fished all night in vain, and Jesus was no fisherman, Peter obeyed and a great catch came in. In John 21 a man whom Peter did not recognise stands on the beach and again tells Peter to let down his empty nets one more time. Oh the beauty of Jesus' heart! Peter has gone back to fishing, gone back to his livelihood because of the shame of his denial. He's given up on his calling as an apostle because in the eyes of the world and in his own eyes he has failed. But Jesus won't give up on Peter. Jesus won't let Peter drift into living disconnected from the truth of how God feels about him. And now as a great catch comes in, Peter recognises the handiwork of his Beloved. It is one of Jesus' classic 'I know you' moments. Peter jumps into the sea and swims to Jesus. Jesus takes him aside and calls him forth into his spiritual identity once more. He asks Peter three times, once for each of the disciple's denials, *"Do you love me?"* (John 21:17) At first Peter is reluctant. He's wrestling with his shame. He's wrestling with his weakness. Finally Peter breaks forth into the truth and exclaims with passion: *"Lord, You know everything; You know that I love You."* (John 21:17) In other words, 'Oh Jesus, you know that at the core of my being I love you! And now I know that that is how you define my success!' In this encounter Jesus is asking Peter to trade in the shame of denial and failure for the truth of how God sees him.

God doesn't see Peter as a denier. God sees the cry of Peter's heart to be a lover of Jesus and counts it as if it were fully mature rather than weak and prone to denial and failure. As the prophet Samuel found out when he went to anoint king David, people look at the outward appearance. The Lord looks at the heart! God is looking at the cry in Peter's heart to be a lover of God and that is what He counts as beautiful and successful. In the same way, God is looking at the cry in your heart to be a lover of Him and that's what He counts as success! God speaks over Peter and John the same truth the bride confesses in Song of Songs 1:5, 'though you are weak and have sinned I call you lovely and beloved!'

THE GLORY OF THE NEW COVENANT

I remember so clearly the day this truth began to hit my heart. The truth that though I am weak, I am lovely to God. Though I fall short often, God defines me by the sincere cry in my heart to overcome. I was in a season of testing. I had gone through a time when God had allowed much to be stripped from my life. I was burnt out and emotionally ill. I had lost my family, my house, my ministry and my job. Yet God still provided for me in this time. He gave me a job in a warehouse putting price labels on books. I felt like I was Joseph in a foreign prison (see Genesis 37-45).

Daily I would cry out to God: 'What am I doing here?' I would stand at a desk for eight hours a day labelling hundreds and hundreds of books. My boss came to me one day. He told me what a great job I was doing. He told me how I was the only one in the warehouse that week to earn a bonus for the number of books I had labelled. I thanked him quietly but as he walked away my whole body beamed with pleasure. My heart swelled and the inner voice we all know so well spoke, "Ah-ha I will redouble my efforts! I bet I'm the fastest in this place!" But then my heart sank. I was finding my success in putting stickers on books? Seriously? I was finding my success in doing something better than everyone else? Memories of all the insecurity and pain this had caused me over the years came flooding back. I was still finding my identity in how well I performed compared to others. I was still finding my source of life in my natural identity. My inner voice cried out to God in this moment. 'Oh God save me from myself. I want my identity to be found in the fact I am the object of Your desire and affection.' And He whispered back, "I like you. I enjoy you. Even in this place of weakness and failure I like you." Suddenly, the truth that though I am weak I am still lovely to God began to break into my heart. Tears came and I was standing in the cavernous workshop weeping helplessly.

This is the truth of the gospel unique under the new covenant. This is what changed forever when

Jesus died on the cross. We no longer have to live from the weakness of our natural identities! We can now live from the definition of who God says we are. And who God says we are is the object of His affection and desire. God says He defines us by the desire of His Son and the righteousness purchased by Jesus on the cross.

When God the Spirit reveals how God the Father and Son define us, when our hearts are moved by the longing of Jesus for us, then something deep within us cries out "Yes!" Something begins to come alive in our hearts. When we are kissed by God's word and moved to transfer the source of our life from our natural identity to our spiritual identity, we begin to come alive on the inside in a way we never thought possible. Then, even in the midst of trouble, our hearts stay steady. Our circumstances, our failures and our weaknesses no longer dictate our success, sense of worth or identity. When we begin to experience this, a bonfire of passion for our Bridegroom ignites in our spirits. The bride in the Song of Songs comes to understand this truth and her statement in chapter 1 verse 5 stands as a prophetic decree that this is a reality available to every person who names the name of Jesus as Lord.

The Song Jesus Sings

THE POWER TO CHANGE

The other stunning result of this spiritual reality hitting our hearts is it actually empowers us to grow and change. In John 8 the Pharisees brought a woman caught in adultery to Jesus. The law commanded she be stoned to death, but they asked Him what He thought hoping to trap Him in His Words. Jesus said, *"Let him who is without sin among you be the first to throw a stone at her."* (John 8:7)

There is stunned silence. Over the next few minutes, the whole company of accusers is convicted and slinks away. *"Jesus stood up and said to her, "Woman, where are they? Has no one condemned you?" She said, "No one, Lord." And Jesus said, "Neither do I condemn you; go, and from now on sin no more.""* (John 8:10, 11) Notice Jesus did not let her off the hook for her sin but through the impact of the forgiveness and redeemed life which He imparted to her He gave this woman the power to change. In the moment when we sin and yet turn the gaze of our hearts to God in repentance to hear His voice saying, 'I define you by the cry in your heart to be mine'. It is there that the power for transformation comes!

PRACTICAL 4: LETTING THIS TRUTH PIERCE OUR HEARTS

King David had this same revelation about God's heart as described in Song of Songs 1:5. If you would like to dive deeper into it read: 1 Samuel 27-31 and Psalm 18. These chapters record a season of David's life when he lived in compromise because of fear. He lived outside the will of God by allying with Israel's enemy, the Philistines, and living in the city of Ziklag. David told many lies in that 16-month season and it caused harm to many people. Yet on the very day he repented and God delivered him, he wrote Psalm 18:19, 20 and 35 - *...He rescued me, because He delighted in me...The Lord dealt with me according to my righteousness; According to the cleanness of my hands He rewarded me... You have given me the shield of Your salvation, and Your right hand supported me, and Your gentleness made me great...* Incredible! In the very minute David returned his life to the ways of God, he knew God put his sin in the sea of forgetfulness, enjoyed him and delivered him because of His affections toward him. David also acknowledges in this Psalm that it is God's gentleness with his weakness which allows him a second (third, fourth and fifth, etc) chance to grow up into the greatness of God's eternal destiny for him.

Practical Exercise

During the time I worked in the warehouse I would turn the promises of the Bible regarding how God viewed me into prayer. I would record these prayers onto my phone and then listen to myself declaring God's promises over myself for hour after hour while I worked. The warehouse became a prayer room for me. Internalising God's promises through meditative prayer is a way we can fill our minds with truth and pile sticks on the bonfire of our hearts as we wait for the Holy Spirit to ignite our passion for Jesus with the Divine Kiss. I have collected a few verses below for you to start with.

Psalm 56:8 – *You have kept count of my tossings; put my tears in your bottle. Are they not in your book?*

Prayer: God you know all the struggles I have been through. You know when I weep and when my heart breaks.

Isaiah 49: 14-16 – *But Zion said, "The* L<small>ORD</small> *has forsaken me; my Lord has forgotten me."*
"Can a woman forget her nursing child, that she should have no compassion on the son of her womb? Even these may forget, yet I will not forget you. Behold, I have engraved

you on the palms of my hands; your walls are continually before me.

Prayer: God my name is written on Your hands. You cannot forget me! You like me and You enjoy me. There is passionate desire in Your heart for me!

Zephaniah 3:17 – *The LORD your God is in your midst, a mighty one who will save; he will rejoice over you with gladness; he will quiet you by his love; he will exult over you with loud singing.*

Prayer: Jesus, you will never leave me nor forsake me. You sing over me with great joy. You have joy in your heart when you look at my life because I am Yours.

Isaiah 64:4 – *From of old no one has heard or perceived by the ear, no eye has seen a God besides you, who acts for those who wait for him.*

Prayer: God even when everything seems hopeless You are still working on my behalf!

Isaiah 40:31 – *...but they who wait for the* LORD *shall renew their strength; they shall mount up with wings like eagles; they shall run and not be weary; they shall walk and not faint.*

Prayer: God, you are the one who will renew my strength! Even in the midst of circumstances that I can't figure out how to solve, You have a way!

Isaiah 62:5 – *For as a young man marries a young woman, so shall your sons marry you, and as the bridegroom rejoices over the bride, so shall your God rejoice over you.*

Prayer: You like me God! You enjoy me! You rejoice over me! I am Your favourite one. The passion in Your heart for me is like the passion of a bridegroom for his bride.

VALUE FIVE

....

EATING THE FRUIT OF JESUS' WORK

Song of Songs 2:3 – As an apple tree among the trees of the forest, so is my beloved among the young men. With great delight I sat in his shadow, and his fruit was sweet to my taste.

To this point I have phrases like: 'the truth of how God feels about us needs to touch our hearts', 'we need to feel what God feels' and 'the Holy Spirit needs to pierce our hearts with truth'. In Song of Songs 2:3 we find the bride comparing the Bridegroom to an apple tree in the middle of a forest. The bride sits under the apple tree and eats its fruit. This image offers a doorway into understanding what those phrases I keep using look like in experience. It is described in Ephesians 1:15-19 as the Spirit of wisdom and revelation:

"For this reason, because I have heard of your faith in the Lord Jesus and your love toward all the saints, I do not cease to give thanks for you, remembering you in my prayers, that the God of our Lord Jesus Christ, the Father of glory, may give you the Spirit of wisdom and of revelation in the knowledge of him, having the eyes of your hearts enlightened, that you may know what is the hope to which he has called you, what are the riches of his glorious inheritance in the saints, and what is the immeasurable greatness of his power toward us who believe, according to the working of his great might..."

God desires for the spiritual eyes of His people to be opened to know Him deeply.

AN APPLE TREE IN A FOREST

Have you ever walked through a pine forest in the middle of a hot summer? It is dark and cool and still. It's as if time stands still when you step under those trees and into a wonderland where it just might be that Narnia really does exist. The only sounds are the crackle of pine needles under foot and the rushing of wind far above. Nothing grows down on the forest floor with little sunlight and soil smothered under needles of pine. Have you ever come across an apple tree in the middle of such a forest? It would be an unusual sight indeed. Yet in verse 3 of chapter 2 the Bride describes Jesus as, *"As an apple tree among the trees of the forest"* in comparison to the sons of men. This comparison describes the unique beauty of Jesus in comparison to all other things in the universe. Psalm 45: 2 echoes this revelation, *"...you (Jesus) are the most handsome of the sons of men."*

For many of you reading this book you have grown up in Christian families, gone to church all your life, graduated from Sunday school and youth group, always believed in Jesus, always read your Bible, worked hard to maintain a quiet time, done ministry inside and outside the church and know a lot of facts about Jesus. But Jesus desires to reveal more than facts to us.

In 2009 I had been working temporary contracts at a University Library, filling in for staff who were on long service and maternity leave. It was my first full-time job and I loved it! The people were fun and easy going. The work was interesting and stretching. The management was supportive and encouraging. I applied for a permanent job in that library. 106 others also applied. Of those, I was one of ten who were chosen for interview. I had the interview and it went very well. As I waited to know whether I had won the position I prayed earnestly for God to move on my behalf. I also made a promise to God with regards to the outcome. I told the Lord, whatever happened, whether I landed the job or not, I would worship Him. The phone rang. Of the 107 applicants I was ranked second. I did not get the job. Tears of disappointment, dismay and confusion ran down my cheeks after I hung up the phone. If I hadn't got an interview at all or if I had been fourth during the interview process that would have been better, but second? What was God doing? It was as if He wanted to disappoint me. But then I remembered my promise. Right there I fell on my knees and began to worship even as the tears of disappointment continued to flow. I think I sang Chris Tomlin's song, *Blessed be Your name.*

5 months passed. I found another job. To be honest, I hated this new job. I was locked away at the top of an 18-story office block photocopying documents for government lawyers. I received a phone call. It was the library. They had decided to open another position and were offering it to me without interview or application. To everyone's surprise, I turned it down. In the months I had been working at the new job I hated, I had started attending a church close to my workplace. While I was attending this church, the Holy Spirit was poured out on a group

of young adults in a way which totally transformed my life. It started me on the journey that now finds me writing this book. God had given me something far better than the job I so wanted. He had given me what I truly desired which was Him. Psalm 37:4 says, *"Delight yourself in the LORD, and he will give you the desires of your heart."* This verse is no longer just words on a page for me. The God who knows my inward being and emotional make up (Psalm 139), who is my good shepherd (John 10; Psalm 23) and who satisfies my desires (Psalm 34) is written on my heart. These verses now move my heart in a way they couldn't before. Now nothing will ever separate me from knowing Him in this way because I have seen him and experienced Him like this.

Job 42:5 – *"I have heard of You by the hearing of the ear; But now my eye sees You."*

TRUE REVELATION

Back in Value 1, I talked about how when we see the beauty of the Lord it causes our hearts to explode with love back towards God. The beauty of the Lord operates in our hearts when the facts we know about God in our minds are taken deep enough by the Holy Spirit to touch our spiritual beings. The natural response is then to have our emotions moved to delight and joy. In other words, we call God beautiful when His work and character are written onto our hearts like they were in my job testimony. This is called revelation. Revelation as described in Ephesians 1:17-19 is not a clever idea or memorable realisation. It is an experience of who God is. It is a spiritual transaction. It is the Holy Spirit revealing God to our heart, mind and emotions and it almost always comes through the Word. When we experience revelation, we will know it and it will change our lives.

Even today, more than five years after the job experience described above, when I read one of the verses I mentioned or hear them read I am reminded of who I know God to be and it brings tears to my eyes and love to my heart. On the flip side, if you've never experienced revelation before it is outside the realm of one's ability to imagine. It can only be pursued by faith and persistence. Yet this pursuit is immensely worthwhile.

The Song Jesus Sings

HIS FRUIT IS SWEET TO MY TASTE

Returning to Song of Songs 2:3, verse three continues: *"With great delight I sat in his shadow, and his fruit was sweet to my taste."* The apple tree represents the work of Jesus on the cross, so rare and precious. Everything God reveals to us about who He is comes as a direct result of the cross and the access to God's heart redemption purchased for us (John 1:18). We see the bride eating the fruit of Jesus' work. She is consuming the beauty of God. This is a powerful image of what revelation is. True revelation happens when we digest the truth of who God is and it becomes part of who we are (see Song of Songs 7:8 as an example – the Bride's very breath now smells of apples). True revelation takes place when we see who God is with the eyes of our hearts and are transformed into His likeness (see 2 Corinthians 3:7-18). Like food which becomes part of our physical bodies once digested, revelation becomes part of our spiritual bodies. No one can ever rob us of the true revelation God gives. It is written upon our inner beings forever, and truly it is sweet to the taste.

EATING THE FRUIT OF JESUS' WORK

SITTING UNDER THE APPLE TREE

Then the bride says, *"I sat..."* She is sitting down, dialing down the busyness of life to sit at the feet of Jesus and delight in eating the fruit of His work and character. She is setting apart time to hear His word, to gaze up at Him and encounter Him. This is what I talked about in Value 3. This is the same posture of heart and life Mary of Bethany takes in Luke 10:39 – *"And she had a sister called Mary, who sat at the Lord's feet and listened to his teaching."*

Today so many Christians are missing out on true revelation. They're not taking the time to sit at Jesus' feet and hear His Word. Most often we accept Jesus as our saviour and immediately rush off to do ministry. We rarely wait to fully digest the fruit of His work and character. Of Mary of Bethany Jesus said, *"...but one thing is necessary. Mary has chosen the good portion, which will not be taken away from her."* Luke 10:42)

As John 15 describes, true ministry comes as the fruit of abiding in Christ. It comes when we sit at His feet. It happens when we eat of His fruit until it becomes part of us. His character becomes our character. His will our will. What He feels we feel. What He thinks we think.

2 Corinthians 2:15 says, "*For we are the aroma of Christ to God among those who are being saved and among those who are perishing...*" Our lives are meant to give off the fragrance of the character and work of Christ to those around us. This is true ministry. The only way we are going to become people like this is to sit at the feet of Jesus in prayer, to take hours to meditate on the Word, to give our lives to radically pursue His beauty. It is only by the knowledge of God becoming beauty to us that true ministry happens.

PRACTICAL 5: DIGESTING THE FRUIT OF JESUS' WORK

Return to your journal and spend some time writing your thoughts and answers to the questions below:

1. Do you have a testimony where God has worked in your life? What truth about God does this testimony reveal about God that is now written on your heart?

2. What are the problems you are currently facing in your life?

3. Ask God to reveal the truth of Himself in these problems. Continue to ask God to do this every day for the next two weeks.

4. When He reveals Himself, as He will, write down your testimony and share it with someone.

VALUE SIX

....

AN INHERITANCE FOR JESUS

Song of Songs 2:10 – My beloved speaks and says to me: "Arise, my love, my beautiful one, and come away…"

There is, before and around the throne of God, a vast sea stretching more endless than the Pacific. It is blue like crystal and glass, clear as an Australian summer sky. It's solid for standing but it's also deep and moving, changing. It's moving with waves and those waves are waves of fiery love and passion.

Under the sea are creatures. They are the kind of creatures you might expect to find in a nightmare. A seemingly convoluted mix of human and animal, four with four faces and four wings each, huge, powerful, burning ones, moving so quickly they appear as flashes of lightning (Cherubim). Yet they are utterly captivating and beautiful beyond description. You cannot take your eyes off them and yet want to hide from their gaze at the same time.

On the sea is a throne of radiant sapphire blue and above the throne fly four more creatures (Seraphim) with 6 wings each, covered in eyes, crying out voices which shake the sea: *"Holy, holy, holy..."* (Isaiah 6:3) From the base of the throne comes a river of fire flowing into the sea to fuel its waves and seven mighty columns of fire that hold still as if to support a roof but then dance across the room which has no visible end, over the sea and back to the throne.

Upon the throne sits the Ancient of Days shining with a light and fire piercing brighter and deeper than any nuclear blast rending even to joints and marrow those who would look upon Him. This light is a white clear light as a diamond yet red as a ruby and surrounded by an emerald green that is only hinted at in the brightest rainbow ever seen on a cloudy day. This scene goes on in heaven hour after hour, day after day, millennia after millennia for eternity in the presence of God. And these are but a few details of the scene experienced by a select few in the Bible.

The Song Jesus Sings

SHOW ME YOUR BEAUTY!

It is amazing how similar the testimonies of these people are in the books they wrote, separated by centuries and millennia. Yet one of these had a slightly different encounter with the heavenly throne room than the others. Moses saw the fire and lightning of God. Moses saw the cloud hiding His throne. Moses heard the thunder and trumpet blast of God's voice. He felt the earth quake beneath His feet. But Moses said, "...*show me Your glory.*" (Exodus 33:18) The Hebrew word translated here as 'glory' is Kabod. Kabod means splendour. Splendour means brilliant or gorgeous appearance. In other words, Moses essentially asked, 'Show me Your beauty!'

God said, *""But," he said, "you cannot see my face, for man shall not see me and live." And the Lord said, "Behold, there is a place by me where you shall stand on the rock, and while my glory passes by I will put you in a cleft of the rock, and I will cover you with my hand until I have passed by. Then I will take away my hand, and you shall see my back, but my face shall not be seen."* (Exodus 33:20-23)

And when God showed Moses His beauty, human history changed forever.

THE BEAUTY OF THE LORD

Properly considered with even an ounce of imagination, the throne room scene is one which fills us with fear and awe at the power and holiness of God. Just imagining the eight living creatures and thinking of coming face to face with one of them is enough to fill one with dread. Yet when God comes to explain to Moses what He is like and what all this glory and power means He doesn't say, 'I am powerful!' He doesn't say, 'I am Holy'. He doesn't say, 'I am to be feared'. God says instead, interpreting and defining what is around His throne, *""The Lord passed before him and proclaimed, "The Lord, the Lord, a God merciful and gracious, slow to anger, and abounding in steadfast love and faithfulness, keeping steadfast love for thousands,[a] forgiving iniquity and transgression and sin..."* (Exodus 34:6, 7)

The first thing God says about Himself and about His beauty is that He likes humans! When Moses asks God to reveal His beauty, God explains His beauty is to be seen in His passion for people. When the almighty, all powerful, all knowing, perfect God comes to define Himself and tell the first thing He wants us to know about Him He says: 'I am merciful, gracious, patient and good to people!' Then Moses responds like all the others who encountered God's throne responded: He "...*quickly bowed his head toward the earth and worshiped.*" (Exodus 34:8)

Could it be that true worship comes from encountering the truth that although God is totally other than humans He has fiery, passionate affection for us? Could it be that all the things God has chosen to reveal about His throne room are telling us about His desire for us? Could it be that the river of fire coming forth from the throne is a river of passion for people (Daniel 7:10)? Could it be that the blast of trumpets from the throne are actually the sound of God singing over us (Zephaniah 3:17)? And could it be that the intensity of the very scene around the throne is giving a picture of how intensely He longs to fully possess the affections of human hearts?

God has inextricably linked the declaration of His glory to fully winning the hearts of the human race. In other words, God has linked the proving of His greatness to His ability to win us as a bride for His Son. For God to fail in this endeavour would be to declare into the eternal that He has some kind of weakness. While God is an almighty, all-powerful God, He uses His immeasurable power FOR LOVE. God uses His power to inspire voluntary, overflowing, all-consuming love in the hearts of people. Jesus will have a bride! The glory and fame of God's name depends upon it! This is the truth into which Song of Songs 2:8-17 delves.

WAITING ON GOD

Western culture and society tells us repeatedly we can have what we want now. The whole of our world is striving to make this a reality – fast-food, fast cash, speed-dating, broadband internet. If you want it, you should be able to have it and have it NOW. Yet, throughout the gospels Jesus tells us again and again to observe the way the natural world is constructed in order to understand His truth and His ways. *"Look at the birds of the air..."* He says in Matthew 6:26 when telling us not to worry about what we will wear and what we will eat.

"...you know how to interpret the appearance of the sky, but you cannot interpret the signs of the times." (Matthew 16:3) he says to the Pharisees of His day. As followers of Christ we need to tune our lives to the ways and rhythms of God.

As opposed to our "fast-food" culture God's work in us is like the passing of seasons. Cold winter days meld into weeks and weeks to months and the changes in the weather seem almost imperceptible from one day to the next. Then, one day, summer comes. In the same way, day after day we live. We come into His presence, meditate on His Word, pray, fast, give, press in to eat the fruit of His work and so often we feel as if nothing is happening. Then one day, the season changes and we have grown. Slowly, imperceptibly, day-by-day God has been changing us from the inside out.

We call this the 'suddenlies' of God. Yet it isn't a 'suddenly' at all. God has been working the whole time. We have simply been unaware of His work and so the change of season surprises us. This change of season is the experience Song of Songs 2:8-17 describes. Over the first chapter and a half of the book, Jesus has been laying a foundation of spiritual identity in the heart of His bride. He has been speaking His unconditional love and affirmation over her and waiting for the cement of this foundation to set solid in her life. This is a critically important season!

In chapter 2:7, the bride gives advice to her friends, the daughters of Jerusalem, saying, do *"not stir up or awaken love until it pleases."* Here she is advising them to tarry long in whatever season God has them and not to move out of it in a hurry. This is such important advice for us! Jesus knows it is vital for us to stay in the King's chamber and under the apple tree, in the place of deep communion, revelation and intimacy until He Himself moves us onward. It is vital to stay in whatever season He has us in until He has finished doing the work He needs to do. God doesn't primarily want bigger and better for us. He wants weaker, deeper and more dependent upon Him. The apostle Paul came to understand this when he heard God say to him about the thorn in his flesh, *"My grace is sufficient for you, for my power is made perfect in weakness."* (2 Corinthians 12:9)

THE BRIDE IS CALLED TO BE JESUS' INHERITANCE

As we have seen, this first season of the bride's journey involved being lavished with the love of God and experiencing the blessings of healing, love, affirmation, restoration and joy. In this initial season He becomes our inheritance and source of life. We come to love Jesus because of what He does for us and what we receive from Him. This is the natural and right response of immature love.

Yet the path to maturity and Christ-likeness, the path into the fullness of all God has planned for our lives involves more than this. The journey the Song of Songs takes us on leads us to understand ourselves as Jesus' inheritance and reward. We are called to become so captured by the beauty of God's heart that we become consumed by what He is consumed by. Pleasing the heart of God and seeing the desires of His heart fulfilled instead of seeking our own blessing becomes our primary motivator. This is where the apostle Paul came to when He wrote, *"For to me to live is Christ, and to die is gain."* (Philippians 1:21) Paul was so consumed with the desire of God's heart for people that he counted even his own life as worthless in comparison to this end.

In chapter 2 verse 8, the Bridegroom now comes skipping effortlessly across the mountains and hills. These mountains and hills represent places of difficult ministry. The bride is startled to encounter Jesus in this way. To this point, she has only ever known Him as the one who blesses her with affection and intimacy and good things under the apple tree. All is well in this place and she feels safe and secure. Yet now in verses 10-14, Jesus gently and reassuringly invites her to come with Him into a new season. It is a season of learning not only to receive His love and blessing but to walk with Him in the difficult places of the earth. It is an invitation to partner alongside Him in ministry as His inheritance and for His inheritance.

God is not looking for servants who would work for Him yet be disconnected from His heart and plan. However, at the same time, He also does not only want us to camp out under the apple tree forever (though we will always come back to this place for respite and sustenance). Rather, Jesus desires that from the place of intimacy we would become consumed by the things which consume Him (namely His longing for people). He is looking for partners who would work alongside Him in the arduous places of the earth to see His desire for a bride fulfilled. Jesus is looking for ones whose ministry would come from the place of ongoing connection to His heart. The biggest difficulty is not the work or the heart-connect. The biggest difficulty is doing the two together. The beautiful truth in this reality is that there are things Jesus has to share with us which He can only share in this place of partnership. Therefore, even the invitation to the mountains and hills is an invitation to deeper intimacy. It is an intimacy the bride has yet to experience.

THE DIFFICULTY OF ENTERING IN

Sadly, in our fast-food, 'now' driven culture, many do not realise the beauty and joy which God wants to give us when we take up this invitation to be His inheritance. Inviting people to sit in prayer and communion hour after hour, day after day, year after year is one of God's strategies to awaken us to this. It is here that God encounters His people. We become consumed by and addicted to going deeper and seeing more of who He is. We begin to hear Jesus' invitation to come away with Him to the mountains and hills. We must have more of His love and so are eventually compelled to follow. If it were not for the season under the apple tree, communing at Jesus' feet, sitting in prayer and encountering His heart, we would never go.

At first, our lack of experience makes this invitation to prayer seem difficult. It appears we are wasting our lives and may sit in a room by ourselves and do nothing forever. Yet the opposite is true. One day Jesus will bring us forth from under the apple tree (Song of Songs 2:8-17 describes this).

At the beginning we see only the cost of sitting at His feet (see Luke 10:38-42) but as we enter in we discover there is such glorious reward. It is a reward of intimacy, joy and delight. It takes a supernatural vision, faith and Holy-Spirit imparted courage to begin. It also involves a change in lifestyle which our culture and society dismisses as boring and a waste of time. Yet it is what we were made for, heart and soul. We were made for communion with our maker far deeper than we have possibly imagined. We were made to be filled with delight, fascination and obsession in our pursuit of His heart and the things which move Him (His inheritance).

Daniel prophesied in chapter 12:3 of his book that those who are wise will shine like the brightness of the galaxy in the night sky and like stars forever and ever. I see this applying to those who go on this Song of Songs journey. Jesus calls us to eternal greatness as His inheritance. His calling starts in the intimate place of the King's chamber and under the apple tree. Then it traverses the difficulty of the mountains and the hills of arduous ministry. As we begin to catch a glimpse of Jesus' heart, His desires become our desires and our cry becomes the same as that of the Moravian missionaries, *"May the Lamb receive the reward of His suffering."* (History of the Moravian Church, Hutton 2008)

THE MOUNTAIN OF SEPARATION

How does the bride respond to Jesus' invitation? In verse 14 she is scared and hides in the clefts of the rock. The intensity of Jesus' zeal as well as fear of the unknown causes her to hide. In verse 17 she gives her answer even as Jesus tells (see verse 14) of His deep longing to see her face and hear her voice:

Verse 14 – Bridegroom to Bride
"O my dove, in the clefts of the rock, in the crannies of the cliff, let me see your face, let me hear your voice, for your voice is sweet, and your face is lovely."

Verse 17 – Bride to Bridegroom
"Until the day breathes and the shadows flee, turn, my beloved, be like a gazelle or a young stag on cleft mountains."

The Hebrew describes the mountains here as 'the mountains of Bether.' The Hebrew word 'Bether' means separation. The bride, in fear and immature faith refuses the invitation of her Beloved.

Yet God is kind. When Jesus comes knocking to invite us to journey with Him into the wilderness of mountains and hills we are always full of fear because we don't know what it will involve. How can we know? It seems like we may be giving up everything for nothing.

We're about to give up what the world says is important and follow Jesus to the ends of the earth or into some ministry which doesn't pay at all. Yet Jesus has given us the Song of Songs to identify with and draw courage from. Being afraid, disliking change, not fully trusting and wanting to stay in the season of safety is part of our story! The Lord knows this. He both understands and has a plan that allows us to overcome.

Would you go on this journey? Would you enter in by beginning to sit at His feet and ask to know His heart? Your King is calling you forth.

The Song Jesus Sings

PRACTICAL 6: ENCOUNTERING GOD'S FEROCIOUS DESIRE

1. Meditate on the throne room scenes in the Bible. Read each of the passages listed below and create either in drawing or words a picture of the throne room from the details given. Ask the Holy Spirit about things you don't understand.

   Ezekiel 1 and 10
   Revelation 4 and 5
   Daniel 7:9-10
   Isaiah 6: 1-10
   Exodus 19, 24, 34

2. Now find and listen to Jon Thurlow's song, *Storm all around You*. You can find it on your preferred download or streaming music service.

3. Throughout this process, ask the Lord what He is revealing about Himself and His desire for you.

VALUE SEVEN

....

THE INFINITE WORTH OF A LOVESICK HEART

Song of Songs 3:1-2 – On my bed by night I sought him whom my soul loves; I sought him, but found him not. I will rise now and go about the city, in the streets and in the squares; I will seek him whom my soul loves. I sought him, but found him not.

I can't speak for the single ladies amongst us but I know as a single man about to turn 32 that as Eric Ludy writes: *"Desire rages within me to have a female companion, someone I can love and be loved by, someone I can be intimate with."* (Eric and Leslie Ludy, When God writes your love story, 1999, p.26)

Have you felt this in your life? Have you loved someone and had them not return your affections? What do you do with that?! Yet here's a more startling question: have you ever felt this kind of longing from and for Jesus? Truly, Jesus put longing in our hearts so that we'd understand a little of His own. Jesus longs to be married to us in the same way a man and woman long to be married to each other. In fact, His longing is far deeper than ours. When we feel His longing for us then we will long for Him. This is the result of sitting under the apple tree and being kissed by His Word in the King's chamber. We'll be changed forever by the wound of love He puts in our hearts.

A DRUG AND AN ADDICTION

Encountering the beauty of Jesus and communing with Him is like taking a highly addictive drug. Once you've tasted a little you'll want more and more. Just like heroin, as we become used to His presence and love, our hearts require more to fill and move them. I used to weep for hours in the gentle presence of God but now my hand and arm shake only slightly (in the presence of the Holy Spirit) as I long for the one who has wounded my heart with a longing so deep I feel sometimes I might burst.

Jesus knows the beauty of His love will become an addiction to us. He knows it will sustain us and spur us on in our pursuit of Him. Incredibly, He always has more. The vastness of God's love for you and me is like the Pacific Ocean and our capacity to take it in like a small plastic cup. God says, 'Come and drink me!' What He has to reveal to us about Himself will never be exhausted. There is more than enough to go around.

LOVESICK SEARCHING

Chapter 3 of Song of Songs starts with, *"On my bed by night I sought him whom my soul loves; I sought him, but found him not. I will rise now and go about the city, in the streets and in the squares; I will seek him whom my soul loves. I sought him, but found him not." (verses 1 and 2)*

Previously, in chapter 2, Jesus invited the bride to go with Him to the difficult place of the mountains and hills, but she refused. He invited her to come and experience new facets of His heart, facets that can only be experienced in the context of partnership in arduous ministry. Yet, she refused. Now He has left her alone. Feeling the desperate ache of her emptiness she looks for Him in the places she communed with Him previously - in the King's chamber and under the apple tree. She does not find Him.

Finally, the ache of a lovesick heart moves her to begin to widen her search. She leaves the secret place of her bed (Matthew 6:6) and goes out into the streets and squares of the city. Streets and squares in this verse symbolise the institutional church.

It is important to distinguish here between the institutional church and the Church of Jesus Christ. Have you ever realised that the bride of Christ is not a building or an organisation but rather ordinary people who are lovesick for Jesus? Our Bridegroom King isn't coming back for a well-run organisation. He cannot be found in programs, buildings, functions or organisational structures. These things are human constructs designed to serve people by providing us with the opportunity to pursue Him more easily. If these constructs do not serve this end, then they have replaced their purpose and become as god. The bride does not find her Beloved in the institutional church (Song of Songs 3:2).

Yet what is important here? Jesus is not angry at the bride's lack of faith and courage in chapter 2. He knows His bride's heart was wounded by His love in the previous chapters. He knows by withdrawing He will provoke her to come searching. And so, in verse 4 Jesus allows Himself to be found. *"Scarcely had I passed them (the watchmen/leaders of the church) when I found him whom my soul loves. I held him, and would not let him go."* (Song of Songs 3:4) These four verses represent only a short time of separation in which it seems as if Jesus is following His bride, watching her from a distance, waiting for her to come searching.

Back in chapter 2:4 the bride described her first season with Jesus like this: *"He brought me to the banqueting house, And his banner over me was love."* Here she compares the bounty of Jesus' loving affection towards her in this first season as a table lavishly set with a banquet of fine food. She also describes, somewhat naively, Jesus' leadership. His banner over her life, as being designed to bring forth love in her heart for Him. In essence she's saying 'the way He leads me (His banner) is always designed to bring forth the maximum love in my heart for Him.' Interestingly, she has not yet been through trials to see how true this statement really is. It is a statement said in faith only. Now in chapter 3, she discovers the truth of her proclamation in 2:4. In this short season of separation, she discovers that Jesus waits for the full ache of lovesickness to be awakened in her heart before He draws close to her again.

BLESSED ARE THE POOR IN SPIRIT

The beatitudes in Matthew 5:3, 4 and 6 describe this same posture of heart that Jesus is seeking to cultivate in the heart of His bride in Song of Songs 3:1-2.

"Blessed are the poor in spirit, for theirs is the kingdom of heaven. Blessed are those who mourn, for they shall be comforted... blessed are those who hunger and thirst for righteousness, for they shall be satisfied..."

Have you ever really considered the Beatitudes? They extol the blessings available to those who are sad. How can this be? Doesn't it go against so much of what is taught in the Western church right now? Most often we are taught we should be happy, healthy, wealthy and content if we are followers of Christ. This, we are told, should be the testimony of our discipleship to Jesus. Yet this is not what the Beatitudes teaches. A thorough examination of scripture will show that this is not what Jesus counts as important at all. Oh, how badly we have been mistaken! This is not what the Bridegroom is looking for in Song of Songs 3. He is looking for the mourning ache of a lovesick heart! He knows that eventually the ache in the bride's heart will move her to obedience, move her to take up her cross and follow Him to the mountains and hills (Song of Songs 2:8). This has been His plan from the beginning.

THE NEW WINE

This plan of our Bridegroom King is more deeply understood by looking at Mark 2:18-22. Jesus calls this plan His new wine. In this passage, the Pharisees come to Jesus and ask, *"Why do John's disciples and the disciples of the Pharisees fast, but Your disciples do not fast?"* Jesus answers, "Can the wedding guests *(friends of the Bridegroom)* fast while the bridegroom is with them? As long as they have the bridegroom with them, they cannot fast. The days will come when the bridegroom is taken away from them, and then they will fast in that day." Jesus then goes on to talk about new wine which cannot be put in old wineskins.

"No one sews a piece of unshrunk cloth on an old garment. If he does, the patch tears away from it, the new from the old, and a worse tear is made. And no one puts new wine into old wineskins. If he does, the wine will burst the skins—and the wine is destroyed, and so are the skins. But new wine is for fresh wineskins."

Have you ever wondered why Jesus would suddenly start talking about wine and wine skins here when He's been talking about fasting? It appears He's changing the subject mid paragraph. But He's not. What He's saying is that previously fasting had been a religious duty required by the law of Moses. Previously, fear and dutiful obligation were the primary motivators for fasting. This was the old wine. But Jesus declares He is bringing new wine. This new wine is the revelation of Jesus as a bridegroom with passionate love for a bride, a love that evokes mourning, fasting and aching lovesickness in return. The motivation to fast is now meant to be a seeking, mourning and aching heart which has been wounded by love. This new wine requires a new way of understanding and following God (a new wineskin). No longer is the law and the fear it brings the primary motivator for obedience. Jesus is saying that now a heart overflowing with lovesickness will move His disciples to fast. Can you begin to see the beauty of Jesus' leadership in this short season of separation in Song of Songs 3? He is motivating His bride with love. He is drawing out of her a response she didn't even realise was already planted in her heart.

Having been restored to her Beloved observe the bride's response as she proclaims with an overflowing heart, *"I held him, and would not let him go until I had brought him into my mother's house, and into the chamber of her who conceived me."* (Song of Songs 3:4) Love has been multiplied in the heart of the bride! How well Jesus knows the movements of her heart! He has done what He planned and His banner over her truly concerns cultivating the deepest love for Him possible.

The mother here again is the institutional church who helped to give spiritual birth to the bride. The bride, having had the ache of love awakened in her heart by even a short separation from her Bridegroom, declares that from now on she will never let Him go. Not only this but she declares she will bring Him and introduce Him to all in her church.

THE INFINITE VALUE OF A LOVESICK HEART

International House of Prayer worship leader Jon Thurlow (Mourning for the Bridegroom, 2010) sings: *"I will embrace the ache of a lovesick heart."* It is a precious ache indeed. Firstly, it causes us to seek after God and position our hearts and lives to find great reward in Him. Hebrews 11:6 says, *"...He rewards those who seek Him."*

Secondly, the ache of being lovesick positions us as poor in spirit, as humble and contrite, as available for God to commune with deeply. The beatitudes in Matthew 5 as well as Isaiah 57:15 express this profound truth.

Isaiah 57:15 says, *"For thus says the One who is high and lifted up, who inhabits eternity, whose name is Holy: "I dwell in the high and holy place, and also with him who is of a contrite and lowly spirit, to revive the spirit of the lowly, and to revive the heart of the contrite.""*

In other words, there are two places God dwells. Firstly, He dwells on His throne in heaven, high and lifted up – unreachable - but He is also close to those who are humble and contrite. When we are wounded by the love of Jesus and begin to ache and mourn for our Bridegroom, that lovesickness brings us to humility and contrition before Him. Jesus is overcome by our lovesick hearts and cannot help but draw close to us.

LONGING FOR THE BRIDEGROOM

Matthew 9: 14-17 and Mark 2:18-22 both tell the same story, *"Can the wedding guests (friends of the Bridegroom) fast while the bridegroom is with them? ... The days will come when the bridegroom is taken away*

from them, and then they will fast in that day."
We are called to long and mourn and fast for Jesus because we are lovesick. Are you lovesick? If not, why not? You can choose to live your faith journey primarily from the motivation of duty and fear of punishment, but it will lead you to live burnt out and disappointed or apathetic. Or you can choose to take up the invitation of the Bridegroom in the Song of Songs and enter into the delight and pleasure of knowing Him and His heart of consuming passion.

The hour we live in is urgent. All the Biblical signs suggest Jesus' return is only, at most, a few decades away. Matthew 24 speaks of a time just before the return of Jesus that will involve a period of persecution for Christians like none seen in history. Matthew 24:22 even explains that unless God were to cut short these comings days no one would survive. Matthew 24:13 gives us the strategy for coming through this impending storm victorious: *"But the one who endures to the end will be saved."*

The book of Revelation describes in greater detail the events outlined in Matthew 24. Of the saints who overcome the tribulation it is written, "*And they have conquered him* (the antichrist) *by the blood of the Lamb and by the word of their testimony, for they loved not their lives even unto death."* (Revelation 12:11)

How can we endure to the end? How can we endure even to the laying down of our lives? We can only do so when we love something or someone else much more than even ourselves. This someone is Jesus. Jesus knows that only a lovesick heart for Him will sustain us through the time of great trial to come. This is another reason Jesus is calling His bride to undertake the Song of Songs journey today. He is inviting us into the journey to gain a lovesick heart. He knows what is coming and He is preparing us as only a tender shepherd and passionate bridegroom would.

PRACTICAL 7: MARRIAGE AS A METAPHOR

In Genesis 2:18–24 the writer of the book tells the creation story and describes how God made woman as a 'helper comparable' to man. The word for 'helper comparable' in Hebrew is Ezer. Throughout the Old Testament the word Ezer is used to describe God. E.g., *Our soul waits for the Lord; He is our help [Ezer] and our shield.* (Psalm 33:20) This word Ezer means 'to rescue, to save or to be strong'. In other words, Genesis 2:18 could be translated as 'I will make man a strength corresponding to him to partner with him so he will not be alone'.

At the end of this Genesis passage, the writer also writes, *"Therefore a man shall leave his father and his mother and hold fast to his wife, and they shall become one flesh."* (Genesis 2:24)

In Ephesians 5:24–31, the apostle Paul, having obviously read this Genesis passage many times, interprets its spiritual significance. He says, quoting Genesis 2, *"'Therefore a man shall leave his father and mother and hold fast to his wife, and the two shall become one flesh.' This mystery is profound, and I am saying that it refers to Christ and the church."* (Ephesians 5:31, 32)

Paul indicates that one of the key reasons God has given marriage is so we would have a taste of the longing and love of His heart towards us. God desires us in the same way we love our husbands and wives or in the way we long to be married (see also Isaiah 62: 4, 5 and Hosea 2:16, 19, 20). In the metaphor of marriage God has gifted the human race a doorway into experiencing the longing of Him for us.

Ponder these questions in your journal and through prayer:

1. If you're married, how do you desire your husband/wife? If you're unmarried, describe your longing for a 'helper comparable'. If you really have no desire for marriage, then ask the Lord what He is saying to you through this chapter

2. Ask the Lord to reveal His heart to you on whatever you have written to the questions above.

3. Go back to the prayers you wrote in Practical 4 and pray them over yourself again. Pray them slowly and ask the Lord again to touch you with His love. Ask Him this question: Jesus, how much do you love me? Would you let me feel your jealous, passionate desire for me?

VALUE EIGHT

....

NOTHING SHALL SEPARATE US

Song of Songs 3:6 – What is that coming up from the wilderness like columns of smoke, perfumed with myrrh and frankincense, with all the fragrant powders of a merchant?

The gospel is not an idea. Rather the gospel is a person (Romans 3:21-26) and the story of this person. The gospel is the author and perfecter of our faith. The gospel is the God who became a man because of His furious longing for people, a longing like the desire of a bridegroom for his bride. Song of Songs 3:6-11 provides one of the most beautiful and deep depictions of the gospel in the entire scripture. In these verses the bride gives a detailed description of how she encounters Jesus when she finds him amidst her lovesick searching in the streets and squares of the city through the previous 5 verses. The bride is now interpreting the encounter with Jesus she has just had in verse 4. She's saying, 'this is how it was when my aching, lovesick heart found my Beloved. This is how I experienced Him to be in that moment.'

WHO IS THIS MAN?!

Verse 6 expresses the awe she felt as Jesus found her. 'What is that?!' She cries. He is seen coming up from the wilderness signaled by the rising dust of a royal procession. The wilderness is always the place of intercession. This is further confirmed by the description of Jesus being perfumed with myrrh and frankincense. Myrrh symbolises suffering and frankincense prayer (see note 3 for details and cross references). It is painful prayer. It's prayer bursting from a heart of overwhelming love for another. The bride is crying out, 'Who is this?! He came up from the wilderness where He had been pouring out His life in intercession before God because of His love for me! Who is this man who would do such a thing?!'

Jesus' death on the cross was the single greatest act of intercession in the history of humankind. The cross was the cry of Jesus' heart made manifest in human action. It was the ultimate expression of His lovesick heart, for His Father and for His people. It was the thunderous cry of a lovesick Bridegroom, 'I want YOU!'

It is from the wilderness of the cross that the Bridegroom comes in verse 6. He has been triumphant in the deepest of pits and fiery trials, the fiercest of wildernesses and now He comes up victorious. His coming up is like a whirlwind from the desert, like a pillar of smoke moving upon the horizon. Where there is smoke there is fire, right? Hebrews 12:29 says, *"Our God is a consuming fire."* Revelation 1:14 describes Jesus' eyes as like a flame of fire. That fire is the flame of desire for His people, the desire driving His passionate heart of intercession. And so, the Bridegroom comes up from the wilderness for His bride. He comes to win and lead His people by His intercession (Hebrews 7:25).

A ROYAL PROCESSION

Song of Songs 3:7-10 continues the story:

"Behold, it is the litter of Solomon! Around it are sixty mighty men, some of the mighty men of Israel, all of them wearing swords and expert in war, each with his sword at his thigh, against terror by night. King Solomon made himself a carriage from the wood of Lebanon. He made its posts of silver, its back of gold, its seat of purple; its interior was inlaid with love by the daughters of Jerusalem."

Verses 7 - 10 here describe how Jesus leads the royal procession, the wedding procession that accompanies Jesus out of the pits of hell. He comes with a couch, a litter, a palanquin.

A palanquin is a portable chair or couch enclosed by curtains and carried by servants. It was used in many ancient cultures as the transport of choice for royalty. This palanquin is made by the king Himself from cedar - the finest, hardest wood in existence. What king makes a palanquin by his own hand or even can make one by his own hand except our carpenter of Nazareth, Jesus? Its pillars are silver, symbolising redemption. From the pillars hang the purple curtains symbolizing royalty inside and out. It is our redemption by Christ which gives us our royal identity (Revelation 5:10). It is not by our birth or our status or our ability that we are royal heirs but only by His work and His choosing. The palanquin's carrying supports are of gold, symbolising divine character. Jesus is working in us to produce divine character and on the day of His wedding He will have a bride who has a heart like His heart.

A THOUSAND MAY FALL BUT IT SHALL NOT COME NEAR US

The palanquin is not alone either. It is surrounded, says verse 8, by sixty warriors, the finest of the finest, the SAS of Jesus' soldiers, warrior angels hardened in battle, each with a sword to protect the bride from the flaming arrows of the evil one (Psalm 91). From the pit of hell, Jesus has ascended and allowed Himself to be found by those who will truly hunger and thirst for Him. He comes to us triumphant, ready to lead, ready to invite us into an adventure of redemption and love leading to the development of divine character and deeper soul connection with Him. He also comes to invite us into a journey in which He will protect our steps until we arrive one day before His throne.

Did you know, as a Christian, that while you are within Jesus' will He will keep your life until your purpose on this earth is complete?

When we were preparing to start the House of Prayer in Australia I spent five months in New Zealand, training at the Tauranga House of Prayer. I arrived at the end of June 2013. It was winter time in New Zealand. Standing on the beach at Mt Maunganui on the day I arrived, I saw an island which looked to be about 300 metres offshore. Something akin to summit fever, the manic drive which spurs mountain climbers to irrationally head for peaks even under threat of incoming blizzards, fell upon me. I determined then that before I left New Zealand I would swim to that island and explore it. Fast forward 5 months and spring had come, the air temperature warmed and it was my last week. I struck out in still frigid seas for the island. Sadly, the swimming distance proved to be further than I thought, well over a kilometre. When I reached the island and walked onto the beach my right calf began to cramp. I thought little of it at that point. However, when I got back into the water and began the return swim both my legs and neck began to cramp badly. Within 10 minutes I was in trouble as my body began to shut down under the onslaught of hypothermia and dehydration. I stopped thrashing for a time to rest and as I lay there on my back with the sun sparkling above me and the water breathing around me I let out a silent prayer: 'Papa, I think I'm in trouble. If you want me to live you're going to have to help.' It was the first time in my life where my body was actually physically unable to obey my brain's command to push on. I looked up from my prayer. A group of kayakers had miraculously appeared to my left. I signalled for help and they towed me to shore. Twenty minutes later I lay on the warm sand covered in blankets, shaking violently, with my legs and back as stiff as a board as the effects of hyperthermia set in. Some people rubbed my blue feet with sand. Others fed me orange juice through a straw. I lolled in and out of consciousness. A young man from the House of Prayer prayed at my shoulder and I began to speak in tongues under the presence of the Holy Spirit. He moved to my feet and prayed again. Bolts of heat shot up my legs as life surged back through my body. God didn't want me to die that day. It was He who sustained me.

I'm not telling this story to encourage people to do irresponsible things but to illustrate that God is watching over His beloved ones. Those 60 mighty warriors from Song of Songs 3:8 are ever present in our lives. The adventure Jesus invites us on in the wilderness is one which is surrounded by His love and His ever-present help until we see Him riding in the sky at the time of His second coming.

THERE'S GOING TO BE A WEDDING

The last verse of chapter 3 describes the bride's revelation regarding the consummation of the gospel. A story without an ending is no story at all and this also holds true for our story with our Bridegroom King.

In his song, <u>More than Ashes</u> (*Let the weak speak*, Merchant Band, 2008) Tim Rhiemerr sings, *"There's going to be a wedding, it's the reason that I'm living, to marry the Lamb."* The wedding day is the point of the gospel. The day Jesus splits the sky and comes to marry His church, is what He died for. I believe on this day, when we finally see our King Jesus face-to-face we will fall at His feet and for literal years proclaim: Holy, Holy, Holy and Worthy, Worthy, Worthy for all He is and all He has done.

"Go out, O daughters of Zion, and look upon King Solomon, with the crown with which his mother crowned him on the day of his wedding, on the day of the gladness of his heart." (Song of Songs 3:11)

Then He will be crowned as King by His Church (mother) and joined inseparably to His people as Bridegroom.

It is why Jesus went into the wilderness of the crucifixion: for the joy of this day set before Him, the day of the gladness of His heart (Hebrews 12:2).

I believe 2 Corinthians 4:16, 17 also describes this day: *"So we do not lose heart. Though our outer self is wasting away, our inner self is being renewed day by day. For this light momentary affliction is preparing for us an eternal weight of glory beyond all comparison."* Do you eagerly and joyfully anticipate the return of Jesus? Is it the focus of your life? Is it your 'blessed hope' (see Titus 2:13)? Be honest. If not, why not? This is not a condemnation, it's an invitation! It's an invitation to press in for the revelation that you are the object of His desire, you are 'the one Jesus loves.' When His desire begins to touch our hearts then our hearts explode with desire for Him in return. This is how we were made to live!

HE WILL HAVE HIS BRIDE

In chapter 3:6-11, the bride has a revelation of the gospel, the height and width and length and depth of the furious love of God from which she cannot be separated. The gospel is a Bridegroom and this Bridegroom will have a bride. This is certain. What is also certain, is it will be a bride who is 'a helper comparable' to Him. (Genesis 2:18) Revelation 19:6 prophesies: *"Then I heard what seemed to be the voice of a great multitude, like the roar of many waters and like the sound of mighty peals of thunder, crying out,*

"Hallelujah! For the Lord our God the Almighty reigns.""

For the first time, the Church actually sounds like Jesus! Revelation 1:15 (see also Ezekiel 43:2 and Psalm 93:4) describe Jesus as sounding like the roar of many waters: *"...His feet were like burnished bronze, refined in a furnace, and His voice was like the roar of many waters."*

Psalm 18:13 (see also John 12:29) describes the voice of God as being like thunder: *"The LORD also thundered in the heavens, and the Most High uttered his voice, hailstones and coals of fire."*

Then Revelation 19:8 says, *""...it was granted her to clothe herself with fine linen, bright and pure"— for the fine linen is the righteous deeds of the saints."*

Now the Church also looks like Jesus!

He is going to do it! His passionate love is enough! His intercession is enough! His loving leadership is enough! Right now, we might look at the state of the church around us and despair at what we see. How could this broken and divided church ever be a bride worthy of Jesus. Yet while we don't know how, and we don't know exactly when, we know the end is assured. Our Bridegroom is coming, and He is coming to remove everything that hinders love in His bride. His bride will be a helper comparable to Him (Genesis 2:18).

PRACTICAL 8: FINDING DELIGHT IN THE WORD OF GOD - PART 2

I'd like to introduce you to another way of meditating on God's Word. This meditation method is based on two premises. Firstly, prayer is meant to be an encounter with God and secondly, the Hebrew definition of meditation is actually 'to mumble over and over again.'

First of all, choose a single verse from Song of Songs chapter 3:6-11 which you understand well and has touched you through this journey. Now follow the instructions below.

1. Choose one short phrase to focus on from the verse you've chosen. For example, here's mine. <u>My chosen verse:</u> Song of Songs 3:6 – *What is that coming up from the wilderness like columns of smoke, perfumed with myrrh and frankincense, with all the fragrant powders of a merchant?* <u>My chosen phrase:</u> **What is that coming up from the wilderness...**

2. Take a page in your journal. Draw four margins on the page about 2 centimetres from the edge of the page – top, bottom, left and right.

3. Prepare your margins
   - In the top margin write your chosen verse and underline or highlight the chosen phrase.
   - In the bottom margin write: Pursuits. This margin is for you to write down any further topics of investigation the Lord gives to you during your meditation time.
   - In the left margin write: Read, Write, Say, Sing, Pray. These are the tasks you are going to do with your chosen phrase during your meditation time.
   - In the right margin write: Distractions. During your meditation time, if you get distracted by something or have a thought that is not on your chosen phrase write it in this margin.

4. Now find a place where you will not be distracted easily. You might like to put on some worship music while you do this. The web stream at www.ihopkc.org/prayerroom is a great resource to use during this kind of meditation.

5. Spend half an hour sitting before the Lord with your chosen phrase. With the phrase follow the instructions you've written in your left margin.

- Read the phrase. Read it over and over again. Change the wording or read the meaning of it not just the exact wording. For example: **'Who are you Jesus? Who is this Bridegroom King?'**
- Write the phrase. Write the phrase over and over. Change the wording. Make it into a story. For example, **'I see a pillar of cloud coming up from the desert.' 'Why is this whirlwind coming up from the desert?' 'Why is there a storming coming out of the wilderness? 'Doesn't a storm usually come from the sea?'**
- Say the phrase. Mutter the phrase over and over again before the Lord.
- Sing the phrase. Turn the phrase into a little song to God.
- Pray the phrase. Thank God for the truth of the phrase. For example, 'Jesus, I thank you that you are the Almighty One

who comes for me with all the strength of a storm'.

6. Finally, it is important to note that this is not a study exercise. The point is not just a greater understanding and knowledge of the passage. The point is encounter with God by the Holy Spirit. Write down what the Lord says to you during this time in the middle space between the margins of your page.

(<u>Revelation by Meditation</u> by Kirk Bennet, https://www.7thunders.org/product/revelation-by-meditation/)

VALUE NINE

....

BEAUTY BESTOWED

Song of Songs 4:12-15 – A garden locked is my sister, my bride, a spring locked, a fountain sealed. Your shoots are an orchard of pomegranates with all choicest fruits, henna with nard, nard and saffron, calamus and cinnamon, with all trees of frankincense, myrrh and aloes, with all choice spices— a garden fountain, a well of living water, and flowing streams from Lebanon.

There is a longing deep down in all of us for beauty. I have never met a person who does not enjoy a stunning sunset, a vast wilderness vista or a white tropical beach. Yet this delight goes deeper even than desiring to behold beauty. We not only want to behold beauty; we long to possess it (Mike Bickle, *Seven Longings of the Human Heart*). Deep at the core of our beings every one of us longs to be beautiful. Truly most of the men amongst us do not say it this way. Nor do the cool, swaggering youth. They call it something different, but they have the same longing. It's the longing to be attractive. Jesus knows this. It was He who buried this longing deep inside of us. It is part of His plan for the journey He longs to take us on.

HIS GENTLENESS MAKES US GREAT

Now as the bride clings to her Beloved (Song of Songs 3:4), having been reunited with Him after her separation, Jesus declares His delight in her despite her immature faith and disobedience when refusing His initial invitation. Chapter 4:1-5 and 7-15 record the Bridegroom calling out the beautiful character traits that He sees beginning to form in His bride. These budding seeds of character are described as a secret garden of spice and oil bearing plants. Here King Jesus speaks of character traits that are mere seeds in the bride's heart, yet He describes them as if they are fully mature. In effect He prophesies over her and delights in not only who she is but who she will be. Jesus is the one who calls things that are not yet as though they are. (Romans 4:7). He sees the beginning from the end. He understands the cry in our heart to love and obey Him as the massive assurance of the maturity to come. He knows the crying out is the beginning of victory even today. The truth is that if He wasn't working in our lives, we wouldn't be crying out and struggling to overcome our weaknesses and failures in the first place. Our awareness of weakness and sin is proof of His power already at work in our lives.

As we saw in Value 8, He comes for His beloved from the wilderness with His mighty warriors and His wedding carriage. He cannot be stopped. Nothing can separate us from His leadership which will surely bring forth mature love in our lives. It is this trait of Jesus' beautiful heart, to relate to us based on who we will be - not only on who we are now, which gives us the strength to mature. David knew this when He wrote in Psalm 18:35, "*...Your gentleness made me great*" and in Psalm 130:3, "*If you, O Lord, should mark iniquities, O Lord, who could stand? But with you there is forgiveness, that you may be feared.*" In essence David says, 'because of my weakness and sinfulness you could wipe me out but because you are gentle to me my heart is empowered to mature.' It's the same truth from chapter 4 again. Though I am dark, weak and prone to failure, You, Jesus, see me as lovely because You define me by the cry in my heart to overcome, rather than my failure. Oh, the transformation this truth will bring when it is written on our hearts!

I WILL GO MY WAY TO MOUNTAINS AND THE HILLS

Then at last, in verse 6, the continued affirmation of Jesus so overwhelms the bride's heart that she accepts His invitation to the mountains and hills. Ephesians 5:29 speaks of how Jesus prepares His bride by nourishing and cherishing her. His cherishing leadership finally wins her to full obedience.

In Song of Songs 2:17, when the bride refused Jesus' initial invitation to the mountains and hills she said, *"Until the day breathes and the shadows flee,"* Now in chapter 4, she uses the same words in her complete surrender to His invitation, *"Until the day breathes and the shadows flee, I will go away to the mountain of myrrh and the hill of frankincense."* (Song of Songs 4:6)

Again, myrrh here represents suffering and frankincense, prayer. The bride is accepting Jesus' invitation to partner with Him in the place of arduous ministry and costly obedience, to share the burdens of His heart in intercession. She is accepting the invitation to be His inheritance. She is accepting the invitation to make the cry of her life: 'my Beloved must receive the reward of His suffering!'

It is a moment which steals Jesus' heart. This one look, this one little yes, though she has not yet even taken one step to act on her words, overwhelms His heart and in verse 7, He prophesies her beauty again.

In verses 9-11, Jesus again proclaims the bride's prophetic identity as the one who has stolen His heart. He says in verse 10, *"How much better is your love than wine..."* Wow! Jesus is saying that the affections of your heart turned towards Him are much more valuable than anything in the entire created order - more valuable than stars and galaxies and mountains and oceans and angels. Then in verses 12-15 Jesus gives a beautiful prophetic picture of what He has been doing, is doing and will continue to do in her heart as she journeys with Him.

A MUDDY HOLE IN THE GROUND

In constructing a skyscraper, the final height is dependent on the depth of foundation initially prepared. The same principle is true in the life of the believer. The more kingdom responsibility God has destined for us to bear (both now and in the age to come), the deeper must be the foundation of our character, Christ-like-ness and identity fixed in Him.

When the construction of a skyscraper begins, it looks like a deep, muddy hole in the ground, a complete mess. In the same way, in those times of struggle, confusion and suffering in our lives, in the spiritual wilderness, we look and feel like a complete mess. But there is something special about this mess, this wilderness, this 'muddy hole' time in our lives.

Hebrews 5:8 says of Jesus, *"Although He was a Son, He learned obedience through what He suffered."* Isaiah 53 makes it clear nobody has ever suffered as much as Jesus did. Yet nobody brought forth as much fruit or ascended to as much glory as Jesus either.

Living in and through seasons of wilderness has a way of deeply impacting people. Wilderness makes us withdraw into ourselves. It forces us to confront the deep, empty well inside our fleshly hearts. It causes us to turn to God for help because we run out of our own strength and ability to cope. In the midst of the wilderness, we start to exercise, build and grow the God-pursuing muscle of our hearts.

In a deep, muddy hole, a foundation for a skyscraper can be built. In the deep well of our hearts found in wilderness and then turned over to our Bridegroom, a garden of Godly character, beautiful beyond anything in the created order, can be planted. The old, fleshly and sinful self is removed and replaced with God's own character and beauty (see Isaiah 61:3). This is the beauty we all long for. Yet when we're in the midst of a difficult season, it's nearly impossible for us to see what God is up to. The bride experiences this. Jesus proclaims over her in verse 12 that she is a garden enclosed, a spring shut up, a fountain sealed. In other words, the beautiful character He has planted in her heart to this point has not yet been revealed (even to her). Now He is going to give her a glimpse of the beauty of His work and the impartation of His very own beauty into her.

Even the bride at this point only sees herself as a 'muddy hole'. In verses 13 and 14 Jesus now reveals 8 different spice and oil bearing plants He has planted in the garden of the bride's heart. Each plant symbolises a precious and beautiful character trait Jesus has carefully cultivated. These traits include: righteousness, consecration, faith, a worshipping heart, a lifestyle of prayer and full abandonment to the ways of God (see Note 3 for a full explanation of the symbols here). Finally, in verse 15, Jesus prophesies that from this point onwards, from this garden of the bride's heart, will come streams of living water to everyone she meets (see John 7:38). To this point, the life of the bride has been hidden. People have only seen her as a mess and a 'muddy hole'. Her life has truly been 'hidden in Christ' but now it is going to be displayed for all to see (Colossians 3:3). Jesus has given the bride His own beauty and now this beauty will be a testimony of the beauty of Jesus to others.

IT'S GOING TO BE WORTH IT

Do you know what it is like to find that the months and years of difficulty and confusion you have endured have not been wasted? Do you know what it is like to find that by walking faithfully through the wilderness season God has stored up within you a rich treasury of beautiful character? That's what Hebrews 12:11 is talking about:

"For the moment all discipline seems painful rather than pleasant, but later it yields the peaceful fruit of righteousness to those who have been trained by it."

The only natural response you can have to this discovery is overwhelming joy. It's why Paul writes in Romans 8:18 – *"For I consider that the sufferings of this present time are not worth comparing with the glory that is to be revealed to us."*

God knows the cost we pay in passing through whatever wilderness we go through in this current age, is nothing compared to the glory (beauty!) awaiting us in the age to come. Then all our doubters and all our mockers and all our accusers will see the true wisdom of our pursuit of Christ! If we will go on the journey Jesus has for us, there will be a day when, no matter what has happened to us, we will proclaim from the very depths of our beings: It was worth it! It was all worth it! God knows this. He really knows. He sees this future day and knows the reward of the beauty He is cultivating in our hearts will dwarf in value even the most extreme suffering we can experience.

AWAKE, O NORTH WIND AND COME, O SOUTH

The well-known missionary-martyr Jim Elliot famously wrote: *"He is no fool who gives up what he cannot keep to gain what he cannot lose."*(Elizabeth Elliot, 2002, *The Journals of Jim Elliot*) This quote echoes the truth that as we have a revelation of the beauty of the reward God has for us, we cannot help but respond in the same way as the bride in verse 16: *"Awake, O north wind, and come, O South wind."*

The north wind in Israel is the rough, cold wind coming in off the desert while the south wind is the warm, gentle wind coming from the sea. The north wind symbolises difficult times while the south wind symbolises times of refreshing. In other words, as the bride catches a glimpse of the incredible work Jesus is doing in her heart she cries out, 'I trust You Jesus. Come suffering, come good times. In whatever circumstances I face I will trust You and proclaim you as good because I have caught a glimpse of Your heart towards me and your work within me. I know you are doing a good work in me. Your banner over my life really is love!'

She continues in verse 16: *"Blow upon my garden, let its spices flow."* In this sentence she is expressing her revelation that true evangelism comes from being a living message of the beauty of Jesus. She is saying: 'Jesus, would the beauty of the character qualities you have planted in me now draw others to know You as I know You?'

Finally, she says: *"Let my beloved come to his garden and eat its choicest fruits."* Here the bride says: 'I'm all Yours Jesus! Everything I have is Yours. I trust You!'

Oh, what a place to come to! What abandonment! It is a place not found by might or will but only by an encounter with the intensity of love, mercy and desire that Jesus has for us over the journey of life. This is the place our Bridegroom King is inviting His people to. He is inviting us to catch a glimpse of the work He is doing in our hearts and to become living gospels about the beauty of Christ. Prayer is the means of entering in. Abandonment to the ways of Jesus unto a testimony of His beauty in the whole earth is the end. And finally, at last, it will be this lovesick abandonment which causes our Bridegroom to split the sky and come home for His people!

Psalm 45:10-11 – *Hear, O daughter, and consider, and incline your ear: forget your people and your father's house, and the king will desire your beauty...*

PRACTICAL 9: BEHOLDING BEAUTY AND BECOMING BEAUTIFUL

When we encounter Jesus' longing and affection for us, we are empowered to overcome the less-than-beautiful areas of our lives. Here is the prayer I recorded and listened to as I tried to fill my mind with the truth of Jesus' heart for me. Take this prayer as an example and create your own prayer to fill your mind with the truth about how God feels about you. As we fill our mind with truth the Holy Spirit opens our hearts to <u>experience</u> truth. Use the promises from Practical 4 to help you.

Here I am Your beloved one, God. I am Your beloved one. I am Your favourite one. I am the one who moves Your heart. Nobody else can move Your heart God the way that I do. I am Your favourite one. I am Your beloved one. I am Your beloved one. I am the one that You are captivated by. I am Your beloved one. God I am Your excellent one in whom is all Your delight. I am Your beloved one. I am Your perfect one. I am Your chosen one. The one for whom You have chosen good things. There is nobody like me God. Nobody else can move Your heart the way that I do. I am Your beloved one. I am Your beloved one. You enjoy me God. You enjoy me God. You enjoy me. I am Your beloved one. I am Your beloved one!

VALUE TEN

....

THE FELLOWSHIP OF HIS SUFFERING

Song of Songs 5:6 – I opened to my beloved, but my beloved had turned and gone. My soul failed me when he spoke. I sought him, but found him not; I called him, but he gave no answer.

In the land of ancient Israel, it was legal to own slaves, yet they had to be set free in the seventh year of their service. However, if a slave, who had served faithfully for six years so loved his master that he wanted to continue to serve then he would become a bondservant (Deuteronomy 15:17). The master was to take an awl and pierce the slaves' ear as a symbol that this man would live for the rest of his life to listen to the will of his master. A bondservant was a servant of love. Motivated by love, he chose to give up his freedom to continue in loving service forever.

In 1 Corinthians (6:19, 20) the apostle Paul writes, *"Or do you not know that your body is a temple of the Holy Spirit within you, whom you have from God? You are not your own, for you were bought with a price."*

Paul understood his life had truly been bought by the priceless blood of Jesus. He knew his life was not his own. He knew that he owed an unpayable debt to Christ (see Romans 1:14). This is the legal position we all find ourselves in as the redeemed of Christ. Our lives are not our own for we are slaves belonging to God. Once we were dead in our sins before God but by the great sacrifice of His Son He redeemed us for Himself. We all know this as gospel 101. Yet God does not primarily want dutiful slaves. He gives us freedom to choose our level of response, even after He has saved us. He will not force us into anything, but God longs with passionate desire for labourers of love, for lovesick bondservants.

In Romans 1:1, Paul describes himself as a bondservant of Christ. God is longing for us to fully commit ourselves to His ways because of our love for Him. Yet the degree to which our hearts respond in love to God is always the degree to which we have experienced His love for us first (see 1 John 4:10).

Christianity is not primarily a faith of sacrifice. First and foremost, it is a faith of response. Our Bridegroom waits for us and woos us with His love, time after time after time. He is patient and He is kind.

In Song of Songs 4:16, this is the place the bride has finally come to. She says: *"Awake O north wind, and come, O south wind! Blow upon my garden, let its spices flow. Let my beloved come to his garden and eat its choicest fruits."* You could say that the bride asks to be a bondservant and for Jesus to come and make her life a testimony, drawing others into the same experience of love and response.

In 5:1, Jesus acknowledges the faith and love of the bride. He acknowledges for the first time the bride's heart and life have been given fully to him and He has come to take possession, by invitation, of what He desires. *"I came to my garden, my sister, my bride, I gathered my myrrh with my spice, I ate my honeycomb with my honey, I drank my wine with my milk."*

Then in this same verse, Jesus invites the Father and the Holy Spirit (His friends) to come and drink deep of the rare love and life in the heart of His bride.

"Eat, friends, drink, and be drunk with love!"

Jesus' commends the bride to the Father and Spirit (the friends). Though the bride has not yet reached full maturity, Jesus proclaims His pleasure and enjoyment in their relationship. Amazing!

IS HE ENOUGH?

Now in chapter 5:2 we find the bride resting. She is peaceful and secure in the love of her Bridegroom. Her heart is awake. She is waiting for His voice, ready for Him to come and lead her to the mountains and hills but not stepping ahead on her own.

"I slept, but my heart was awake..."

Jesus now comes to test and prove her, to find out the depth of refined character and love within her. He comes to find out whether this is a bride who is in it for Him, and Him alone. 'Am I enough?' is the question He comes to find an answer to. 'If the bride loses all, will she love me for me or is she only in it for what I can do for her?' Proven character and love becomes the true witness of the beauty and majesty of Jesus and the great power of His loving leadership in our lives. As the internal fruit of the bride's life comes under the pressure of circumstances, the fragrance of her response bursts forth to all who know her. This fragrance is such a testimony to those around her that many souls are won to Christ. In this season, Jesus not only tests her but simultaneously answers her request to be a testimony of His goodness from 4:16.

THE MOUNTAIN OF MYRRH AND THE HILL OF FRANKINCENSE

The Bridegroom begins this season of testing by knocking on the door of the bride's heart (5:2).

"...A sound! My beloved is knocking. "Open to me, my sister, my love, my dove, my perfect one..."

Now that she has said yes (4:6), He invites her to allow Him to share with her the deepest longings of His own heart. Later we discover the deepest longing of His heart is for those who are lost. We discover the bride already knows this (6:2, 3).

In 5:2 we observe that as Jesus comes to His bride His head is covered with dew.

"...for my head is wet with dew, my locks with the drops of the night."

He comes from the garden of Gethsemane, from watching and praying through the hours of the night. The Bridegroom has come now to take the bride to the mountain of myrrh and the hill of frankincense. The mountain of myrrh and the hill of frankincense is the place of arduous ministry, costly obedience and suffering intercession. It is the place of sharing in the 'myrrh' of Jesus' longing for a bride, the place of partnering with Him in persistent, difficult prayer for the Church and of labouring alongside Him in the difficult work of calling the lost home.

JESUS LIVES TO MAKE INTERCESSION

In Philippians 3:8-10, Paul writes, *"Indeed, I count everything as loss because of the surpassing worth of knowing Christ Jesus my Lord...that I may know Him and the power of His resurrection, and may share His sufferings* **(the fellowship of His suffering)**, *becoming like Him in his death that by any means possible I may attain the resurrection from the dead."*

Paul is giving us a glimpse into the depth of what Jesus is inviting His bride to in Song of Songs 5.

The Song Jesus Sings

Have you ever had an intense experience in a foreign country or culture? Did you come back to your home culture and explain your adventure to the blank stares of misunderstanding loved-ones? This is what soldiers experience when they come home from war. There is no one with whom they can relate. There is no one who understands. In the crucible of terrifying violence and hardship shared with their mates they have formed such a bond and depth of unique experience that they find even loved-ones don't 'get it'. When you came back to your own culture to the shock of being misunderstood it was probably those ones with similar experiences with whom you connected best. This experience gives us insight into the experience and invitation of Jesus in chapter 5 and the fellowship of suffering described by Paul.

In the garden of Gethsemane, Jesus longed for someone to watch and pray with Him and found no one. As a man, He longed not to be alone in His hour of greatest need. He says to Peter, James and John, *"So, could you not watch with Me one hour?"* (Matthew 26:40) In the garden, I believe He began to feel the weight of humanity's sin and brokenness which He was to bear on the cross.

Hebrews 12:2 describes how Jesus despised the shame of the cross. He didn't want to go through it.

He cried out in the garden, "*My Father, if it be possible, let this cup pass from me...*" (Matthew 26: 39). Yet His passion and longing for a bride (see John 17:24) as well as His love for His Father drove Him on. "*My Father, if this cannot pass unless I drink it, your will be done.*" (Matthew 26:42).

He was caught between two powerful yet opposing forces – the force of furious desire and love and the natural human longing for self-preservation. In the midst of His struggle, He longed for ones who would understand Him. This was the intercession of Jesus. He stood as an intermediary between the Father and humanity. His love brought reconciliation between the two and cost Him everything. In the midst of this trial He longed for someone to understand and even today He still longs.

This is similar to the experience of the bride in Song of Songs 5. Firstly, with a responsive heart, she rises to take up her Beloved's invitation (v.3-5).

I had put off my garment; how could I put it on? I had bathed my feet; how could I soil them? My beloved put his hand to the latch, and my heart was thrilled within me. I arose to open to my beloved, and my hands dripped with myrrh, my fingers with liquid myrrh, on the handles of the bolt.

Her questions regarding her robes are rhetorical in nature. Robes throughout the Bible are used to symbolise righteousness (Revelation 19:8; Isaiah 61:10; Matthew 22:12; Revelation 3:4). She has taken off her own filthy robes and been clothed with Jesus' own righteousness. While reading verse 3 it may seem she is reluctant to take up Jesus' invitation, yet the opposite is actually true. In essence she is saying: 'I truly believe I have already taken off my dirty robes and been clothed with righteousness, how can I even think about putting them back on again by refusing your invitation? I am all in." When considered alongside her cry of 4:16 this understanding rings true.

In verse 4 she opens the door of her heart to allow Jesus to share with her the longing of His heart. As she opens the door of her heart and allows herself to feel just a little of the passion of Jesus' desire for the lost (the myrrh she finds on the handle of the lock left there by the Bridegroom's own hand – v. 4, 5) Jesus removes His discernible, tangible presence. This doesn't mean He has abandoned her completely, for the Holy Spirit always lives in the spirit of the believer. Rather it means she no longer feels Him close. She can't see where He's leading or what He's doing in her life.

Now again (as in chapter 3:1-5) the bride searches for her Beloved but does not find Him (5:6). She cries out for Him but hears no answer (v.6). Again the watchmen (leaders in the church) find her (v.7). This is the second time they have found the bride searching, longing and crying out for her Bridegroom. The first time in chapter 3 they passed her by. Now they turn on her in indignation and condemnation. The very ones who should be protecting her, nurturing her and championing her dedicated, radical pursuit of Jesus are the ones who come against her. It is often from the very ones who should understand us that we receive the deepest wounds. The watchmen condemn and humiliate her. They also strip her of her ministry (her veil). These leaders in the church are fed up with her passion and radical pursuit. They want her to calm down and live like all the other pew sitters in their church.

Was this not also the experience of Jesus? In His three years of ministry the ones who knew Biblical prophecy and the signs of the times best were the Scribes and Pharisees. The ones who should have most easily recognised Him were these. Yet it was the Scribes and Pharisees who rejected Him most completely and persecuted Him most violently. On the night Jesus prayed in the garden it was one of His own disciples who betrayed Him into their hands. Hanging on the cross the next day Jesus cried out, *"My God, my God, why have you forsaken me?"* (Psalm 22: 1) This is the cry echoed by the bride in 5:6: *"I opened to my beloved, but my beloved had turned and gone. My soul failed me when he spoke. I sought him, but found him not; I called him, but he gave no answer."*

Not only does Jesus remove His presence from the bride but persecution and difficulty have also come to her life now.

Thus, the bride has lost much, though not yet her own life. She stands at a crossroads in her faith. She stands caught between two powerful yet opposing forces –the natural human desire for self-preservation and the suffering longing of lovesickness for her Bridegroom.

THE FELLOWSHIP OF HIS SUFFERING

Hebrews 7:25 says, *"Consequently, He is able to save to the uttermost those who draw near to God through Him, since He always lives to make intercession for them."* From the day Jesus ascended to the right hand of the Father 2000 years ago, He has lived to intercede on behalf of His bride on the earth. He longs for us to partner with Him in this. Jesus stands as a great high priest for humanity. Right this minute He stands in the gap between the Father and people. His overwhelming love for His Father keeps His eyes upward and His overwhelming love for people keeps His hands reaching out to us, drawing the two parties together.

It is in and through the invitation to open our hearts to feel Jesus' burden, and the difficulty which inevitably comes from saying yes to this, that Jesus invites us to go deeper in relationship with Him. In sharing this burden, in accepting Jesus' invitation to Gethsemane, to the mountains and the hills, we find ourselves in a new depth of intimacy. This is the kind of intimacy soldiers share with their platoons. It is the fellowship of suffering. When you pray, *'Awake, O north wind and come, O south wind'*, (Song of Songs 4:16) He allows us to feel a little of the burden of His heart for a broken world, to experience a little of the journey of persecution He experienced. And when you feel what He feels and experience what He experienced there is a connection between you and Jesus which is like nothing else you've ever known. Like brothers on the battlefield He is now able to share with you the deeper things of His heart. Now we begin to experience the pleasure of being close to His heart. I believe He cries out over us at this point, 'Thank you, thank you! I have wanted to share these things with someone but I haven't found anyone who understands me. There are so few.'

Paul describes this in Philippians 3. He has experienced the fellowship that comes with sharing in the sufferings of Christ. He has experienced it in such a powerful way that He is not scared to count everything as loss to experience it again. In our time, our Bridegroom searches for ones who would long to know Him like this, who would long to share the burdens of His heart like this. Today, Jesus is looking for friends.

PRACTICAL 10: THE FELLOWSHIP OF SUFFERING

Using the meditation method outlined in Practical 8, meditate on Philippians 3: 7-11.

But whatever gain I had, I counted as loss for the sake of Christ. Indeed, I count everything as loss because of the surpassing worth of knowing Christ Jesus my Lord. For his sake I have suffered the loss of all things and count them as rubbish, in order that I may gain Christ and be found in him, not having a righteousness of my own that comes from the law, but that which comes through faith in Christ, the righteousness from God that depends on faith— that I may know him and the power of his resurrection, and may share his sufferings, becoming like him in his death, that by any means possible I may attain the resurrection from the dead.

VALUE ELEVEN

WHAT TO DO WITH SUFFERING

Song of Songs 5:10 – My beloved is radiant and ruddy, distinguished among ten thousand.

What do we do with suffering? It is a question which plagues all of humanity. If there really is a God who is all powerful and yet also full of love, mercy and furious desire for people, then why does suffering exist? Why does He allow it?

Suffering affects everyone. No one is immune. It is the great equalizer. Suffering touches every part of life whether you're a follower of Jesus or not. Whether you're rich, poor, healthy, live in the Sahara desert or New York City.

WHAT TO DO WITH SUFFERING

What do we do with it? As followers of Christ, how do we carry our hearts in the midst of it? When suffering comes we naturally ask that famous question: Where is God in all of this? If we don't know the answer and if we don't know where He is and what He's up to then we naturally begin to draw some very destructive conclusions about His character. This is why Jesus' End Time prophecy of Matthew 24:10, 12 says: *"And then many will fall away and betray one another and hate one another... the love of many will grow cold."*

He's talking about disciples here. He's talking about Christians. When Matthew 24 happens, many will ask the question: 'Where is God in all of this? Why is He allowing this?' And the answers they find within will not hold them steady through this time.

We need to be ready to carry our hearts wisely on that day. We need to be ready to stand as a testimony of His goodness and His ongoing leadership even in the midst of seeming chaos. Song of Songs 4:16 – 6:2 gives a picture of how we can carry our hearts through crisis and difficulty.

The Song Jesus Sings
AT THE CROSSROADS

The bride stands at a crossroads in her faith journey. She has said 'yes' to the invitation of the Bridegroom (4:6) yet now, in chapter 5, the sincerity and strength of this 'yes' is being tested. She hovers near the edge of our narrow, difficult road of faith (Matthew 7:14). I picture all of heaven leaning over the balcony of the eternal, holding its breath and waiting to see her response.

This moment is not only a test of the bride's heart but a test of Jesus' leadership. Has He prepared her well enough for the test? Will she stand in such a time as this? In the good times it is easy to proclaim, *Awake, O north wind and come, O south wind!* When we feel Jesus close and experience His blessings it is easy to make promises about loving Him completely and giving up everything for Him. Yet when difficulty comes those promises are tested. God has a way of testing us (and through this testing, growing us) in places we can never foresee. It can bring us to our knees! The bride stands at the crossroads of the knowledge of God. She is being tempted to ask those famous questions: 'Where is God in all of this? If He really is an all-powerful God who uses His power for love, then why am I going through this? Is Jesus really a passionate Bridegroom? Are His promises really true? Is He really leading well?' She is tempted to doubt His love. In the moment of testing, it is so easy to answer no to those questions. This will be the test for the corporate bride in the days to come.

Matthew 24:9 and 22 make it clear that tribulation and persecution against the world-wide church is coming and will be so severe that unless God cuts it short, none will survive. At this crossroads, how will we respond? In that hour, the question requiring an answer will be: Is Jesus' enough? When everything we hold dear is stripped from us, are we in it for Him? It is then that the time we have spent with Him in the intimate chamber and under the apple tree will be seen as wisdom. It is then that the beauty of Jesus' leadership in leading us to sit at His feet will truly be understood. At the end of it all, only true love will stand the test (1 Corinthians 13:2).

THE BRIDE'S RESPONSE

Between verses 8 and 16, the bride's answer comes forth. In the midst of suffering, persecution, confusion and longing, she does not complain or doubt. She does not question. Her focus is unwavering. Her heart stands true and she cries out for all to hear: *"...if you find my beloved...tell him I am sick with love!"* (Song of Songs 5:8) It's not: 'If you find my Beloved...ask Him why this is happening?' It's not: 'If you find my Beloved...tell Him I'm disappointed.' NO! It is: *"If you find my beloved...tell him I am sick with love!"* This verse is paralleled by the experience of Stephen as he was being stoned in Acts 7. Even as the crowd abused him, Stephen saw Jesus standing at the right hand of the Father in heaven. Even as the stones crushed his body, love filled his heart and burst forth in a request for the forgiveness of his murderers. *"Lord, do not hold this sin against them. And when he had said this, he fell asleep."* (Acts 7:60)

Here is truth. This is the greatest expression of the fragrance of Jesus' work in our hearts.

"Greater love has no one than this, that someone lay down his life for his friends." (John 15:13)

This is the highest expression of love - when, in the midst of "dying" (whether it be actual physical death or the loss of things precious to us) we are still found lovesick for Jesus.

In this the beauty and worth of Jesus manifests through our lives. True evangelism and a faithful witness looks like this. It's also one of the key reasons why the Church grows rapidly in nations where followers of Christ are persecuted. In the midst of persecution only those who really know and love Him stand. When they do stand, a powerful, faithful testimony goes forth.

In verse 9, the Daughters of Jerusalem now enquire with awe and wonder, *"What is your beloved more than another beloved, O most beautiful among women? What is your beloved more than another beloved, that you thus adjure us?"*

In other words, they're saying: 'who is this One called Jesus and what is He like that causes you to respond like this?' The bride doesn't need to preach or try to convince - instead they come and ask her. She has become a living testimony of Jesus' love and leadership. Her very life is now the message of His extraordinary character. Her response to suffering is so other-worldly that it captures her friends' attention and they ask her to explain how she can respond like this.

HIS HEAD IS FINEST GOLD

Now from verses 10-16, the bride answers those who question her with a bold proclamation of her intimate, experiential knowledge of the Bridegroom. It is a glorious ten-fold description of who Jesus is, from the top of His head to the tip of His toes and the beauty of His heart in between [See Note 3 for a full explanation]. It starts with, *"My beloved is radiant and ruddy, distinguished among ten thousand."* (5:10) In other words, Jesus is both God (gloriously white and radiant) and human (ruddy with the healthy complexion of humanity). There is no one like Him (*"distinguished among ten thousand"* (5:10))! *"His head is the finest gold"* (5:11). His head symbolises His leadership and gold speaks of perfection. Even in the midst of persecution and trial (which Jesus could have stopped because He is the Almighty One) she believes His leadership to be perfect and leading her into the fullness of love. The bride concludes with this glorious summary; *"...he is altogether desirable, This is my beloved, And this is my friend, O daughters of Jerusalem."* (5:16) She extolls the beauty of Jesus! She says there is not one ounce of offense or disappointment or resentment in her heart because of the things He has allowed her to go through. He truly is her Beloved and her friend!

The bride overcomes. She validates the perfection of Jesus' leadership and work in her heart. She has truly become a bride who can be equally yoked to the Lion of the Tribe of Judah.

So often throughout history there have been testimonies of mass conversions after martyrdom. Jim Elliot flew as a missionary to the jungle Indians of Ecuador and was murdered by the very ones he went to preach to. Two years later his wife and daughter moved to live amongst the same people who had killed Elliot. They brought many of these same Indians to know Jesus (*Through the Gates of Splendour*, Elizabeth Elliot, 1981). This is in alignment with what Jesus said in John 12:24, *"...unless a grain of wheat falls into the earth and dies, it remains alone; but if it dies, it bears much fruit."*

TRUE EVANGELISM

In Song of Songs 6:1, the Daughters of Jerusalem become the fruit of the bride's season of sacrifice (even as the bride is the fruit of Jesus' sacrifice) as they declare their desire to seek after Jesus also. *"Where has your beloved gone, O most beautiful among women? Where has your beloved turned, that we may seek him with you?"*

The bride responds, revealing that, though in her own life she has been unable to feel Jesus' presence, she knows He is to be found in the harvest field. He is to be found tending to the hearts of young believers who are just beginning the journey of seeking Him out as the bride has.

"My beloved has gone down to his garden to the beds of spices, to graze in the gardens and to gather lilies." (Song of Songs 6:2, 3)

Here the bride is confessing the truth that the purpose of the journey is about raising up the bride. Jesus does not exist only to bless us and give us what we need and want (though He does do that). The point is not that we would be happily lovesick (though that is surely our destiny). The point of our journey is that the Lamb would receive the reward of His suffering! The goal is the satisfaction and fulfilment of the burning desire of Jesus' heart unto the glory and knowledge of God filling the whole universe (Ephesians 3:10). Therefore, this is where our Beloved is to be found, wooing His flock in the harvest field.

Friends, we're living in the middle of a beautiful love story. It's the love story from which all the other love stories ever written find their inspiration. Jesus is after a bride and this bride is not just you or me or even you AND me, it is a corporate bride from every tongue and tribe and people and nation (Revelation 5:9, 10)!

WHAT TO DO WITH SUFFERING

VICTORIOUS IN LOVE

In Song of Songs 6:4 the Bridegroom now comes to meet the bride after her time of testing. Have you ever wondered what it would be like to meet Jesus after you've died as a faithful martyr or after serving faithfully for decades in secret? Oh, glory of glories! Oh, wonder of wonders! Oh, unspeakable joy! *"Well done, good and faithful servant..."* (Matthew 25:23) on its own doesn't quite cut it. We have overcome! We have said no to many tempting detours! We have persevered through wilderness and war and pain and heartbreak and obscurity and loss for the joy set before us! And now our Beloved has come for us!

The closest thing in our earthly experience is the very large, joyous wedding of two lovers who have been in a long-distance relationship for a very long time. It will be the most joyful celebration in history. I believe we will be so overcome by joy we will fall down and worship for a literal hundred years on that day. And after that? We'll feast, and we'll dance!

Have you ever wondered what it was like on the day Jesus met His Father in the throne room after His ascension from the cross? A small picture of this scene is captured in Psalm 24:7-10,

Lift up your heads, O gates! And be lifted up, O ancient doors, that the King of glory may come in. Who is this King

of glory? The Lord, strong and mighty, the Lord, mighty in battle! Lift up your heads, O gates! And lift them up, O ancient doors, that the King of glory may come in. Who is this King of glory? The Lord of hosts, he is the King of glory!

Let this passage sink in. Let it fill your mind and heart and flow deep inside you. What comes out in response?

Returning now to Song of Songs 6:4, Jesus proclaims the bride to be beautiful in physical appearance (Tirzah) and stunning in internal (and eternal) heart (Jerusalem). He describes her as like an army coming home victorious from battle. The army is raising its victory banners!

"You are beautiful as Tirzah, my love, lovely as Jerusalem, awesome as an army with banners."

The Bridegroom is totally overwhelmed by her love and devotion to Him, *"Turn away your eyes from me, for they overwhelm me..."* (6:5) There is none like her He declares, *"My dove, my perfect one, is the only one, the only one of her mother, pure* (favourite) *to her who bore her."* (6:9)

WHAT TO DO WITH SUFFERING

WHERE DID THE BRIDE'S VICTORY COME FROM?

So where did the bride's victory come from? How was she able to stand in the face of so much heartache and confusion and proclaim with no complaint or offense or disappointment or bitterness: *"My beloved is radiant and ruddy, distinguished among ten thousand, His head is the finest gold..."*? (Song of Songs 5:10, 11)

The birthplace of her response to testing was her experiential knowledge of Jesus' beautiful character (chapters 1-5). Because of her previous encounters and the deep foundation of love cemented in her heart, she was able to stand in the unshakable knowledge of who He is.

She remembered the kisses of His Word and the delight of digesting His fruit under the shade of the apple tree. She remembered how He called her beautiful even though she was weak and burnt out and fallen into sin. She remembered how, though she did not take up His initial invitation to the difficult places, He came to search for her with a palanquin surrounded by mighty warriors. She remembered how, even in her weakness, He loved and cherished her and bestowed upon her His own beauty.

In Ephesians 5: 24-32, the apostle Paul gives us a glimpse into Jesus' strategy to raise up an equally-yoked bride, a helper comparable (Genesis 2:18) for Himself. He writes, ...*Christ loved the church and gave himself up for her, that* ***He might sanctify her, having cleansed her by the washing of water with the word***, *so that He might present the church to Himself in splendour,* ***without spot or wrinkle or any such thing***, *that she might be holy and without blemish. In the same way husbands should love their wives as their own bodies. He who loves his wife loves himself. For no one ever hated his own flesh,* ***but nourishes and cherishes it, just as Christ does the church***," (Ephesians 5:25-29)

In other words, nourishing and cherishing the bride by washing her with the kisses of His Word is Jesus' strategy. Nourishing and cherishing His bride by continually speaking over her His love and delight is what we have watched the Bridegroom do from Song of Songs 1 through 4. Chapter 5:10-16 is the fruit of this journey.

WHAT TO DO WITH SUFFERING?

Finally, to answer the question: what to do with suffering? It is this. We need to go on the journey of the Song of Songs. Seriously! Today, this is what the

Spirit is saying to the Church across the earth. It is time to stop business as usual. It is time to gather together in the place of prayer to seek the heart of our Bridegroom through His Word. We need to know what He's like! We have to know how He feels about us! We need to know how He leads, the beauty His heart, the fellowship of His suffering and the power of His resurrection. We need to be close enough to Him to feel the burdens that He carries.

The hour is late. Time is running out for us to be ready. When the crisis soon to hit the planet breaks like a wave upon us, a witness of the beauty, worth and perfect leadership of Jesus will need to be seen. In the coming hour, the harvest field will be ripe in a way never before seen in history. Only a revelation of His burning heart for us will sustain us victorious and faithful in those days.

PRACTICAL 11: THE PILGRIMAGE WE'RE INVITED ON

Using the meditation method outlined in Practical 8, spend time meditating on Psalm 84:5-7:

Blessed are those whose strength is in you, in whose heart are the highways to Zion. As they go through the Valley of Baca they make it a place of springs; the early rain also covers it with pools. They go from strength to strength; each one appears before God in Zion.

VALUE TWELVE

....

THERE IS MORE!

Song of Songs 7: 10 – I am my beloved's, and his desire is for me.

The bride draws towards the end of her journey. From this point on there is never again a separation between bride and Bridegroom. They have become one - one in heart and mind. The bride now feels as the Bridegroom feels and thinks as He thinks. She has accepted the Bridegroom's invitation to the place of suffering intercession, to bear the burdens of Jesus' heart as His partner and has gone down to the harvest field to be with Him (chapter 6:11, 12). Is this not the goal of our Christian journey? We are called as Christians to enter into the very family of God. Romans 8:16-18 says, *"The Spirit himself bears witness with our spirit that we are children of God, and if children, then heirs—heirs of God and fellow heirs* with Christ, provided we suffer with him in order that we may also be glorified with him."

We are invited as brothers and sisters of Christ to enter into the fellowship of the Trinity and it is the Holy Spirit's witness inside of us as a seal upon our hearts which authenticates this identity. Jesus lived as a man this way, *"So Jesus said to them, "Truly, truly, I say to you, the Son can do nothing of his own accord, but only what he sees the Father doing. For whatever the Father does, that the Son does likewise."* (John 5:19)

Jesus lived in constant communion and dependence upon His Father. This is also the way the apostle Paul lived (Galatians 2:20), *"I have been crucified with Christ. It is no longer I who live, but Christ who lives in me.* In Song of Songs 7:10 we understand the bride has also come into this reality and depth of intimacy, *"I am my beloved's, and his desire is for me."*

MY BELOVED IS MINE

There are three verses throughout the Song of Songs which follow the pattern of chapter 7:10. These three declarations of love and longing offer a stunning insight into the growth of the bride's heart along her journey.

In chapter 2:16 the bride proclaimed: "*My beloved is mine, and I am His.*" Here the bride is in the primary position. "*My beloved is mine*"... is her first statement. Then she adds, almost as an afterthought, 'oh yes... "*and I am His.*"' At this point, Jesus is primarily her inheritance and reward, the power of God for the benefit of her own life. This is entirely Biblical and appropriate for the stage of the journey she is in. Psalm 103:2-3 says, "*Bless the Lord, O my soul, and forget not all his benefits, who forgives all your iniquity, who heals all your diseases...*" The same Psalmist goes on to say, "*For He knows our frame; He remembers that we are dust.*" (Psalm 103:14) Jesus knows we are weak. He knows we need to see His goodness in the land of the living (Psalm 27:13). He understands the journey we must go on to discover the depth of His love. Jesus knows the foundation of all our growth is based on the foundation of our experience of His love for us first (1 John 4:10). However, He also longs that we would not become satisfied and stagnant in our journey but would go on to seek maturity. Psalm 84:5 says, "*...Blessed are those...in whose heart are the highways to Zion...*" and Paul in Ephesians 4:11-15 writes,

"*And he gave the apostles, the prophets, the evangelists, the shepherds and teachers, to equip the saints for the work of ministry...until we all attain to the unity of the faith and of the knowledge of the Son of God, to mature manhood, to the measure of the stature of the fullness of Christ, so that we may no longer be children... Rather, speaking the truth in love, we are to grow up in every way into him who is the head, into Christ,"*

The goal of our journey in this life is to grow up into *"...the measure of the stature of the fullness of Christ..."*! (Ephesians 4:15) Wow! In other words, the goal of our journey and the intent of God's leadership over us, is for us to become a bride comparable to the Bridegroom King. Experiencing the blessings, goodness and love of God toward us is always the foundation of the journey but it is not the end. There is more - more joy, more life, more intimacy, more power, more grace, more adventure, more sacrifice. So much more! The reality of who God is and how much He wants to give us is as vast as the ocean. Our capacity to take it in and absorb it is like a little plastic cup. Jesus invites us to bring our cup to Him and start to drink.

I AM MY BELOVED'S

Now in 6:3 the bride proclaims again, *"I am my beloved's And my beloved is mine."* Notice here the order has switched. This time, first and foremost, the bride is Jesus' inheritance, *"... I am my beloved's..."* and then afterwards He is hers, "*...and my beloved is mine...*". The bride is clearly growing and maturing though there is still a hint of immaturity in her second statement as she repeats a line from 2: 16.

HIS DESIRE IS FOR ME

Finally, we come to 7:10 and the statement is very different from 2:16. In 7:10, notice there is nothing in the bride's statement regarding what she is going to gain.

"I am my beloved's, and His desire is for me."

She says, 'I belong to Jesus and His desire is for all of me'. I belong to Jesus because His desire is for me. I am giving my life to satisfy the desire of my Beloved's heart and He Himself, He only, is my exceedingly great reward (Genesis 15:1).

Meditate on this thought for a while! The bride has been so caught up in the furious love and longing of Jesus's heart for her and the lost that she has forgotten about herself. This is not a striving to be selfless. This is a forgetting of self. This is a heart fully captured and lost in love. This is not something we try hard to become. This is where Jesus leads us when we say yes to the journey He has for us. This becomes the natural reflex and overflow of our hearts as we digest the revelation of the beauty of His heart.

MINISTRY OUT OF INTIMACY

The bride started her journey tending the vineyards of other people's hearts and burning out (Song of Songs 1:5, 6 – See Value 4). She burnt out in ministry because she wasn't connected to the life-source of Jesus' love. Then she went through a season of sitting under the apple tree, enjoying the fruit and blessings of Jesus' work on the cross. She left the ministry and went to the secret place of deep communion and intimacy (chapter 1:8-2:7). She concluded that if ministry was the place where burn out happened, and the secret place was the place where her heart burned with love, then she was going to stay in the secret place. But from chapter 2:8 – 6:11 Jesus invited her out from the comfort zone and gently wooed her into the harvest field not to work on her own but to work alongside Him as His equally-yoked helper, as His helper comparable (Genesis 2:18 and Ephesians 5:26, 27).

God is not looking only for workers. He is looking for partners who are lovesick for Him. From chapter 7:1-9, the Bridegroom now equips the bride with ministry tools (see Note 3 for more details) and in chapter 7:10 we find the bride fully equipped for her eternal destiny at Jesus' side. Jesus knows there is a depth of relationship and heart connection He can only experience with His people when He and they are working together with hearts and minds as one. How He longs for this intimacy! And so begins this new season of partnership as the bride proclaims, taking the Bridegroom's hand and leading Him to the place of deeper intimacy, *"Come, my beloved, let us go out into the fields and lodge in the villages; let us go out early to the vineyards and see whether the vines have budded, whether the grape blossoms have opened and the pomegranates are in bloom. There I will give you my love."* (Song of Songs 7:11, 12)

THERE IS MORE!

Have you ever read the writings of Paul and wondered how He can write things like, *"But whatever gain I had, I counted as loss for the sake of Christ."*? (Philippians 3:7) Or what about this one, *"Rejoice always, pray without ceasing."* (1 Thessalonians 5:16, 17) Have you ever thought perhaps Paul wasn't quite a hundred percent serious? Did he really mean those things? But what about God Himself in Leviticus 20:26, quoted again in 1 Peter 1:16 saying, – "...*You shall be holy, for I am holy...*" Is this even possible you may have asked? How does one pray without ceasing? How does one count all things as loss for the sole reason of the reward of knowing Jesus more? Maybe the Bible is only saying these things to spur us to be the best we can be? We often conclude in our minds and hearts (whether we realise it or not) that Jesus and Paul can't really be serious, and we settle into resignation because we don't understand. As we've observed the journey of the bride through the last few chapters, questions like this may have arisen in your heart. Maybe you've been feeling that these experiences the bride has are so far outside of your own experience or knowledge that they're not possible. I exhort you that this is not so! Rather I am entirely convinced the Bible is being serious when it says, "pray without ceasing" and "Be holy as I am holy." It is possible.

Every command in the Bible is possible to fulfil, but not in our own strength or by our own understanding. Every promise in the Bible is possible to experience by persistently saying yes to Jesus when He comes knocking on the door of our hearts. It's not simply a matter of knowing the right thing and then training ourselves to do the right thing. It's a journey into love we must go through. We must go on a journey to become one with Christ. We must follow in the footsteps of our Lord. We must learn to walk as He walks, see as He sees, think as He thinks and speak as He speaks. We need to learn to press in, to ask, seek and knock for more grace, more revelation, more breakthrough, more encounters with His love for us. So often we do not have eyes to see what is available in God because we've never heard of anyone else doing it. We've been shut up in our holy huddles settling for the ordinary and mediocre. We haven't allowed ourselves to desire and dream based on the Word and promises of God in the Bible, or even the experiences of great men of faith through Church history.

Hear the testimony of the revivalist Charles Finney:

"'I could fill a volume with the history of my own experience: an observation with respect to this power that comes from God. It is a fact of consciousness and observation, but it is a great mystery. I have said that sometimes a look, the countenance of a man that has God's power in it, will do more than many, many words. Let me illustrate this fact. I once preached for the first time in a manufacturing village. The next morning I went into the manufacturing establishment to view its operation and to see the factory. As I passed into the weaving department, I beheld a great

company of young women, some of whom I observed were looking at me. Then they were looking at each other in a manner that indicated a trifling spirit. They obviously knew me. They had been at the meeting the night before. I, however, knew none of them. As I approached nearer and nearer to them, their manifestations of lightness began to decrease. This made a particular impression upon me. I stopped and looked at them . . . My whole mind was absorbed with the senses of their guilt and danger. As I settled my countenance upon them, I observed that one of them became very agitated as I stared at her. A thread broke. She attempted to mend it, but her hands began to tremble in such a manner that she couldn't do it. I immediately observed that the sensation was spreading through the factory. It had become universal among all those [girls who were] triflers. I looked steadily at them until one after another, they gave up and paid no more attention to their weaving looms. They began to fall on their knees. The influence spread throughout the whole factory. I had not spoken a word yet. The noise of the looms would have prevented my being heard if I had. "In a few minutes all the work was abandoned. Tears and lamentation filled the room. I had said nothing. At this moment the owner of the factory, who himself was an unconverted man, came in. When the owner saw the state of things, he said to the superintendents, 'Stop the mill,' when he saw what seemed to pierce him in his own heart. 'This is more important,' he *said, 'that these souls should be saved than this mill should be run.' "As soon as the noise of the machinery had ceased, the owner inquired: 'What must I do to be saved? Let us go to the mule room.' So we brought the whole group to the mule room"*—whatever the mule room is. He says, *"It was a marvellous meeting. I prayed with them. I gave them such instructions this time that they could hardly bear it. The word was with power. Many expressed hope in Christ that day. Within a few days, as I was informed, nearly every person in the place was saved with the power of God. This power is a great marvel.""* (Power from on high, Charles Finney, 1872)

And what we do is jump up and down and roll on the floor and laugh a bit and then say we're experiencing revival?! The truth is we have barely seen anything of what God has made available to us. Surely, it is true what C.S. Lewis wrote in his book <u>The Weight of Glory</u> (p.1): *"Indeed, if we consider the unblushing promises of reward and the staggering nature of the rewards promised in the Gospels, it would seem that Our Lord finds our desires, not too strong, but too weak. We are half-hearted creatures, fooling about with drink and sex and ambition when infinite joy is offered us, like an ignorant child who wants to go on making mud pies in a slum because he cannot imagine what is meant by the offer of a holiday at the sea. We are far too easily pleased."*

This is not a rebuke, it's an invitation! The realities of the God are within the reach of ordinary, everyday people. Let today be the day this changes in our lives because God is making something available that is far greater than what we have yet asked for.

SPIRITUAL VIOLENCE

What is it going to take to enter in to this reality? In Genesis 32:22-32, Jacob wrestled with God. Nobody had ever seen God face-to-face and lived - yet Jacob did. Here, about God, it is written,

"When the man [God] *saw that he did not prevail against Jacob... he* [God] *said, "Let me go, for the day has broken." But Jacob said, "I will not let you go unless you bless me.""* (Genesis 32:25, 26)

This is the kind of attitude needed to journey deep into all God has for us. In Matthew 11:12 Jesus said, *"From the days of John the Baptist until now the kingdom of heaven has suffered violence, and the violent take it by force."* We need to have spiritual violence and aggression to take hold of everything that God has promised! We need to stand and say: 'No God, You promised this and I am not going to settle for anything less. I am going to wrestle with You until You bless me even if I die in the wrestle.' 'Even if I DIE in the wrestle' – this is the key! When we pray this prayer in the will of God (note: praying it in the will of God is critically important) I believe God empowers us with the grace to take hold of Him and not let go until He answers our prayer.

In Luke 18:1-8, Jesus tells the parable of the persistent widow. He tells how a widow who was being unjustly treated went to a wicked judge in her city who did not even know or fear God. She persistently asked for him to do his job in bringing forth justice in her case. Because of her persistence, and not because of his own sense of justice, the judge acted on her request. Jesus concludes the parable by saying, *"And will not God give justice to his elect, who cry to him day and night? Will he delay long over them? I tell you, he will give justice to them speedily."* (Luke 18:7-8)

Here Jesus links the persistent, violent and aggressive prayers of His people with the pouring of His power upon the earth. Do you see the connections? Across the world right now God is raising up intercessors whose vision is to see the establishment of persistent day and night prayer. The reality of Luke 18 and the outpouring of power that is promised therein are upon us. This is the invitation to our generation today. Oh, that we would have the humility to step into all Jesus has for us and to go on the journey to become a bride who would give her life to satisfy the desires of His heart. It will require spiritual hunger and violence to go on this journey but the rewards are eternal and glorious!

The Song Jesus Sings

PRACTICAL 12: PRESSING IN FOR THE FULLNESS OF ALL GOD HAS

1. Do a search for all of the Bible passages related to persistent prayer. Here are some to start with: Luke 18, Genesis 32, Matthew 11:11, 12, Matthew 5:6.

2. Ask the Lord for revelation into what He is saying to you through these passages.

3. What do you want? What desires do you have? In what part of your life do you long for breakthrough? Commit to press in with spiritual violence until you see breakthrough. Write down a plan in your journal for how you are going to do this.

VALUE THIRTEEN

INTERCESSION AND THE RETURN OF THE KING

Song of Songs 8:5 — Who is that coming up from the wilderness, leaning on her beloved? Under the apple tree I awakened you. There your mother was in labour with you; there she who bore you was in labour.

In the final chapter of the Song of Songs we see the full beauty of a life surrendered. A relative of the bride asks with surprise and awe in her voice: *"Who is that coming up from the wilderness, leaning upon her beloved?"* It is not even the Daughters of Jerusalem who notice the beauty of the bride but someone else who has not been journeying with the bride at all. It is now clear to all that she is fully dependent on

Jesus. She truly has become the message of Jesus' Bridegroom heart.

SEASONS OF WILDERNESS

As we have seen, the journey of a Christian from first love to total dependence involves passing through many seasons of wilderness. A spiritual wilderness is a season of life where little seems to make sense and the leadership of God is difficult to understand or perceive. These seasons force us to press into God in a way we never would otherwise. They cause us to work the muscle of seeking and relying on God in a more intense way because of the weight of perceived distance those seasons bring. In the desperation of these seasons the wilderness actually becomes the place of encounter with Jesus. The wilderness becomes the place where Jesus woos us as His bride. There is no other path to maturity. Consider this passage from Hosea,

""Therefore, behold, I will allure her, and bring her into the wilderness, and speak tenderly to her. And there I will give her her vineyards and make the Valley of Achor a door of hope. And there she shall answer as in the days of her youth, as at the time when she came out of the land of Egypt." "And in that day," declares the Lord, "you will call

me 'My Husband,' and no longer will you call me 'My Baal [master]."'" (Hosea 2:14-16)

Think of anyone who God used in the Bible. All had seasons of spiritual wilderness during which God refined them into humility and dependence. Take Joseph as an example (Genesis 37-50). At the beginning of his story, he boldly proclaimed his dreams to his brothers inspiring jealousy and betrayal. Sold into slavery in Egypt he rose to prominence in the house of Potiphar only to be falsely accused and thrown into jail. Despite languishing in jail, he again rose to a position of responsibility in the jail itself. Years passed and the butler and baker to the king of Egypt found themselves in prison with Joseph. They had dreams and brought them to Joseph for interpretation. His response to them is profound in revealing the journey of his heart and the slow process of maturation we must all take. *"And Joseph said to them, "Do not interpretations belong to God?""* Joseph is beginning to learn to depend on God. But he is not yet fully dependent for next he says, *"Please tell them to me."* (Genesis 40:8). Though he knows God is the one who gives interpretation of dreams, that God is the provider of all things, this truth has not yet penetrated his heart and he still takes credit for his gift. Joseph interprets the dreams accurately.

Two years pass, and Joseph continues to languish in prison. Do you ever feel that God has you in a difficult place, in a place which is going nowhere? Surely, Joseph must have despaired many times. I can imagine him crying out to the Lord, 'God, what are you doing to my life? What have I done wrong? Whatever happened to all those dreams I had when I was young?' I tremble as I write this next sentence, yet I know it to be true... it's a beautiful place to be! It's the place where the garden described in Song of Songs 4:10-16 (see Value 9: Beauty Bestowed) gets planted in a believer's heart. The garden is planted because God can draw near to us in our humility and desperate searching for Him. Then, when the time is right, as if from nowhere, He can launch us into prominence and fruitfulness. He knows we will never go back to the season of doing things on our own. In the midst of the wilderness it feels impossible that anything could come of our lives, but God knows best.

After two years, the butler, having been restored to his job before Pharaoh, remembers Joseph and tells Pharaoh. I can imagine Joseph awoke that morning to another day of duty and monotony in prison. However, by day's end God had brought Him out of the wilderness, from the prison to the palace in a single day!

How does Joseph carry himself now? How has God worked on His heart in those two years? His response is profound. To Pharaoh's request for the interpretation of his own dream Joseph says, *"It is not in me; God will give Pharaoh a favourable answer."* (Genesis 41:16) Isn't this beautiful? Can you see the journey Joseph has taken? He started by boasting about his dreams of greatness and strength (see Genesis 37:5-8) and now he denies all ability to interpret dreams in his own strength.

This journey mirrors what God found in David's heart as described in 1 Samuel 16:1-13 (Value 1). It also mirrors the journey of the bride in Song of Songs. She starts with herself in the first place, *"My beloved is mine, and I am his..."* (Song of Songs 2:16) Again it is important to reiterate this is part of the journey, it's not wrong. However, she ends with everything being about Him, *"I am my beloved's, and His desire is for me."* (Song of Songs 7:10) Thus Jesus brings her up from the wilderness leaning upon Him.

Why does God take His children on such an arduous journey? It's because He knows that until He has completely won our hearts to dependant love we will never handle the work He wants to accomplish through us. The glory and grandeur He wants us to be a part of would destroy us. We fallen human beings have such a tendency to take glory for ourselves in all things, to make idols of anything and everything. Isaiah 42:8 says, *"I am the Lord; that is my name; my glory I give to no other, nor my praise to carved idols."* God will not share His glory with anyone. A part of this glory is the full affection of our hearts given to Him, and only Him. Thus, our good Father and our Bridegroom long to take us on the journey of the bride in Song of Songs. Though circumstantially difficult, it's a journey which will awaken our heart to abundant life and joy. Isaiah 42:3 says, *"...a bruised reed he will not break, and a faintly burning wick he will not quench; he will faithfully bring forth justice."* He is always gentle yet unrelenting. God prepared Joseph well. Even after years as the governor of Egypt, the greatest empire in the world at the time, Joseph was not corrupted by the power and wealth entrusted to him (Genesis 50:20, 21 and 1 Peter 2:23, 24). God knows our emotional make up and He knows how to bring forth the greatest love in our hearts and dependence upon Him. The journey He has ready for each of us is exactly right. The cross He has designed for us is a perfect fit (Luke 9:23). If we will give ourselves to this journey He will bring us up from the wilderness, leaning upon our Beloved.

The Song Jesus Sings

TRUE INTERCESSION

The rest of chapter 8 verse 5 describes the divine partnership resulting from the bride and Bridegroom being equally yoked and inseparable in mind and heart. The love of the bride for the Bridegroom has now reached a similar level of intensity and maturity to the love of the Bridegroom for the bride. This is what it means to be equally yoked. Jesus gives a hundred percent of His affection toward us and He longs for us to give a hundred percent affection in response. Our hundred percent is much, much smaller than His hundred percent but it is still a hundred percent.

The remainder of the verse says, *"Under the apple tree I awakened you. There your mother was in labour with you; there she who bore you was in labour."*

In many languages, the spelling and pronunciation of certain words differs depending on the gender of the subject being referred to. For example, in Arabic if you ask a woman the question, "How are you?" You must say, "Kif Halek?" However, if you ask a man the same question, you must say, "Kif Halak?" It is the same in French. The word "the" is spelled "le" when referring to the masculine and "la" when referring to the feminine. For example, 'the boy' is written 'le garçon' and 'the girl' is written 'la fille'.

When looking at the Hebrew of the Song of Songs, it is interesting to notice the word "you" in this verse (8:5) is in the masculine form. In other words, the "you" is referring to the Bridegroom and the "I" to the bride (see Amplified version). This is profound. *"Under the apple tree I* [the bride] *awakened you* [the Bridegroom]. *There your* [the Bridegroom's] *mother was in labour for you* [the Bridegroom]; *There she who bore you* [the Bridegroom] *was in labour."*

In these phrases, the bride acknowledges why she has been able to come so far in the journey. She also explains the details of her calling to partner with Jesus in His work on the earth.

As mentioned previously, the mother refers to the church (see Note 3 for a detailed explanation). In Song of Songs 8:5 the mother is seen as being in labour to give birth to Christ in the bride. In other words, the bride is acknowledging that someone in her church has laboured in intercession to see her birthed into intimacy with Jesus.

One of the greatest intercessors in history was Moses. Numbers 11:11-12 describes his intercession–

Moses said to the Lord, "Why have you dealt ill with your servant? And why have I not found favour in your sight, that you lay the burden of all this people on me? Did I conceive all this people? Did I give them birth, that you should say to me, 'Carry them in your bosom, as a nurse carries a nursing child,' to the land that you swore to give their fathers?"

This passage describes intercession in a similar way to Song of Songs 8:5. Intercession is not only the prayers we pray but also involves carrying in our hearts and our bodies the burden Jesus feels for certain issues or people UNTIL His will is birthed into reality. Song of Songs 8:5 intercession involves carrying Jesus' burden in prayer for as long as it takes for His will to be birthed into a situation.

Another way of describing this would be to 'awaken Jesus'. It implies a period of difficult labour even as a mother gives birth to a child. Isaiah 62:6 and 7 describes this, *"You who put the Lord in remembrance, take no rest, and give him no rest until He establishes..."* as does Luke 18:7 and 8, *"And will not God give justice to his elect, who cry to him day and night? Will he delay long over them? I tell you, he will give justice to them speedily."* (see also Galatians 6:19) Entering into intercession like this can only be done by drawing close and experiencing the heart of Jesus. This experiencing comes by sitting under the apple tree and receiving the fruit of His love.

Here in the second half of Song of Songs 8:5, the bride is explaining how she knows she has only come this far in the journey because of the intimate, arduous intercession of others. Now she declares that she too is joining their ranks to partner with the burdens of Jesus' heart. She is not just signing up to pray, she is signing up to carry the burden of His heart even unto death (see Exodus 32:32). This is her response to love.

INTERCESSION AND THE RETURN OF THE KING

We have come full circle. We started with the significance of Jesus' longing for us (see Value 2 – the beauty of longing) and now we end with the significance of our longing for Him.

God is looking for lovesick intercessors. That is the work He is calling us to. He is looking for those who will sit under the apple tree and give their lives to see His will 'awakened' and birthed on the earth (see 2 Chronicles 16:9 and Galatians 6:19). Without agreement from intercessors God's plan will not come to pass. Jesus will not return.

In Revelation 5:8 the four living creatures and 24 elders who live and gaze and worship and pray around the throne of God are seen to hold golden bowls full of incense. Notice what this incense represents:

"And when he had taken the scroll, the four living creatures and the twenty-four elders fell down before the Lamb, each holding a harp, and **golden bowls full of incense**, which are the prayers of the saints."

The incense in the golden bowls is the intercession of you and me. Stunning!

Later in Revelation 8:3-5, this incense of prayer is offered on an altar before God by an angel who then throws a censer of fire from this same altar upon the earth. This fire becomes *"...peals of thunder, rumblings, flashes of lightning, and an earthquake."*

Finally, in Revelation 15:7-16:1 the golden bowls appear again,

*And one of the four living creatures gave to the seven angels **seven golden bowls** full of the wrath of God who lives forever and ever, and the sanctuary was filled with smoke from the glory of God and from his power, and no one could enter the sanctuary until the seven plagues of the seven angels were finished. Then I heard a loud voice from the temple telling the seven angels, "**Go and pour out on the earth the seven bowls of the wrath of God.**"*

Have you noticed? There is a connection between the prayers of the saints (incense in the golden bowls) and the unleashing of God's judgements in these passages. The incense in the golden bowls becomes the wrath of God poured out upon the earth. The prayers of the saints before God actually releases His judgements. The church is called to partner with God's end time plan through intercession.

As the Church begins to become a bride under the apple tree, begins to partner with the heart of Jesus in intercession and cries out to the Father for the day of the wedding, God responds. He starts to shake the earth in answer to the cry of His people. He uses the shaking to call people into the bride and to bring her to full maturity. As the corporate bride increases in size, devotion and fervency of intercession, the shaking upon the earth grows greater in response to the increasing cries of the saints for justice.

2 Peter 3:9 says, *"The Lord is not slow to fulfill his promise as some count slowness, but is patient toward you, not wishing that any should perish, but that all should reach repentance."*

Yes, God is patient and He increases the pressure slowly. Yet He knows that unless humanity is shaken from its comfort and apathy it will not turn to Him. Isaiah 26:9 says, *"For when your judgments are in the earth, the inhabitants of the world learn righteousness."*

Surely, the judgements of God are His mercy towards humanity. They are the last resort of His furious love. He would rather people go through suffering unto salvation than remain in prosperity unto eternal damnation. God's judgements both cleanse the earth of sin; and mature the bride simultaneously until all who can be saved are saved. Then Jesus will split the sky and come home.

Thus, as the coming of our Lord grows close, as the prophesied signs are fulfilled, God is raising up intercessors. Those who would cry out for justice, for the maturity of the bride (both in numbers and depth of intimacy) and the coming of the wedding day.

Prayer is the means of entering into this end time plan of God. The Song of Songs is the roadmap of the journey that prayer takes us on. The goal is the rending of the heavens and the return of the King to a celebration and a future foreshadowed by every wedding day in the history of men and women on the earth.

Like a young man who longs for the day of his wedding but does not knows when it will be, Jesus stands now at the right hand of His Father. His cry of intercession goes like this, 'Father, I desire that my people would be with me where I am. Papa, how long?' (John 17:24) He's waiting for a bride who will respond to His cry. He is waiting for a bride who will call and sing and pray Him home!

PRACTICAL 13: ENCOUNTERING GOD

There are three things necessary for the journey of pressing in for a life changing encounter with God. True, there are times when He comes sovereignly and encounters us by His own choice. But we can also choose to seek after Him in passionate pursuit of more. If we are to walk into the fullness of what He has for us, then this is what we must do.

1. We need to have a question we want God to answer, a breakthrough we need, a prayer we want answered or a promise we want fulfilled. It needs to be something important to us. Our longing for this will keep us going when we might be tempted to give up.

2. We need to fill our minds and hearts with the truth of who God is. The truth in our minds and hearts is like sticks on the bonfires of our hearts. The truth gives the Holy Spirit something to work with when He comes and lights us on fire with passion for God. Filling our mind with truth involves: prayer, meditation, Bible reading, study and listening to Biblical teaching.

3. We need to be persistent. We need to take a stand on what we believe God has for us and determine we will not move until He answers us. This is the most difficult part. This is the part many people don't ever do. This is the part where, when we are tempted to give up on pressing in to God, we must say instead, 'No even if it kills me God, I am not going to stop asking, seeking and knocking. You promised this God. This is my inheritance and I am not going to let go until you bless me with Yourself.' If you undertake these steps above I guarantee that sooner or later, you will have a profound and life changing encounter Jesus. Would you set your heart on pilgrimage today (Psalm 84:5-7)?

CONCLUSION

JESUS' LOVE SONG

So there it is, the Song of Songs - a profound and beautiful song straight from the heart of God. Through this guide, I feel as though I've barely brushed the surface of the profound and beautiful aspects of Jesus' heart. Even as I wrote I felt each Value deserved an entire book of its own. Yet I pray that what is written here will whet your appetite for more and cause you to go on the journey for yourself.

As an allegory of God's love for His people the Song of Songs is not new. It doesn't present any revelation or truth not already in the Word of God. But what is glorious about the Song is its compact nature. It is the whole Bible compacted into 8 chapters. It is the emotions, thoughts and feelings of God in a few short verses. No other single section of the Bible has so much revelation about how God feels

CONCLUSION

toward His people. The Song of Songs has layers and depth and meaning we will meditate on for millennia because, I believe, it's the love song Jesus is singing right now at the right hand of the Father. It truly is The Song Jesus sings.

YOUR ONE WILD, PRECIOUS AND BEAUTIFUL LIFE

The poet Mary Oliver (The Summer Day, 1992) wrote, *"Tell me what it is that you plan to do with your one wild and precious life?"* In our secular world there are many worthy causes to give our lives to. Even in Christendom across the globe, worthy ministries abound... ministries that God is using in powerful ways. Yet you only have one wild, precious and beautiful life and you only get to spend it once.

In Luke 10 we find the story of a woman whom Jesus commended for giving her life to a worthy cause. In this story, Jesus was a guest at the house of Martha in the town of Bethany. In a time and culture where women were expected to serve, Martha's sister, Mary, did not lift a finger to help her sister prepare the food. Instead Mary sat at Jesus' feet and listened to His Words. Mary defied her culture. She defied her gender and her family. Of Mary, Martha complained, *"Lord, do you not care that my sister has left me to serve alone? Tell her then to help me."* (Luke 10:40) Jesus' response resounds through the ages, *"Martha, Martha, you are anxious and troubled about many things, but one thing is necessary. Mary has chosen the good portion, which will not be taken away from her."* (Luke 10:41-42)

Mary knew something and saw something which caused her to live counter to the expectations of those around her. These were powerful expectations, expectations that most would give in to. But Mary's focus was fixed, her gaze sure, her heart lost in the delight of knowing Jesus. Jesus' commendation of Mary echoes David's life vision in Psalm 27:4 to gaze upon the beauty of the Lord all the days of his life. Mary had tasted of the goodness of the heart of God and it was enough.

As the days of this age grow old and the time of Jesus' second coming nears, He invites us to ask ourselves again: what is most important?

Amidst a generation that is the most distracted in history, offered more choice in life than ever before, Jesus invites us to sit at His feet and be kissed by the affections of His heart. He invites us to discover what Mary knew. He invites us to discover a love so satisfying the voices of our culture, friends and families will fade before the One with eyes of fiery passion. We're going to need this love in the days that are coming. We're going to need to live for things other than the approval of our culture, friends and family if we're going to stand faithful.

Later in the story of Jesus' ministry, Mary takes a jar of spikenard (worth a year's wages) and pours it on His feet (see Matthew 26:6-13). This jar was perhaps her entire inheritance and she poured it out, wasted it, on the lowliest part of Jesus' body. Again, Mary is rebuked for wasting something precious which could have been sold for the benefit of the poor. Yet again, Jesus comes to her defence, *"Why do you trouble the woman? For she has done a beautiful thing to me. For you always have the poor with you, but you will not always have me."* (Matthew 26:10-11)

It is much debated whether the story of anointing in Matthew 26 and John 12 are the same but from a comparison of the elements of each story it would seem highly likely. And Jesus goes on to say of this extravagant act of worship, love and sacrifice, *"Truly, I say to you, wherever this gospel is proclaimed in the whole world, what she has done will also be told in memory of her."* (Matthew 26:13)

The way Mary lived didn't make sense to the people around her. The life-vision she had - to know and love Jesus extravagantly - didn't make sense in the context of what could be seen with natural eyes.

The Song Jesus Sings

In the same way, how Jesus is inviting us to live won't make sense to the people around us or in the context of what can be seen with natural eyes. But one day very soon it will make sense. One day soon, like Noah who was ridiculed for building an ark for a hundred years when no one had ever seen rain, the way of Mary, the way of David, the journey of the Song of Songs will be seen as wisdom (Matthew 24:37). For those who take up this invitation be assured there are great spiritual and emotional riches in store amidst the seasons of wilderness. And as I walk this path, praying you too would come away with our Beloved, one verse continues to resound through my heart and mind: *"But, as it is written, "What no eye has seen, nor ear heard, nor the heart of man imagined, what God has prepared for those who love him."* (1 Corinthians 2:9) He is good. He can be trusted. And His desire is for YOU.

NOTE 1

AN OUTLINE OF THE SONG OF SOLOMON

<u>Introduction</u> – 1:1 – 1:4a

The cry for intimacy – 1:2 – the bride cries out for Jesus to touch her with His love.

First encounter with Jesus' love – 1:3, 4a - Jesus answers the cry of the bride and takes her into the chamber of intimacy.

<u>Season 1</u>: **The wilderness of burnout – forsaking first love** - 1:4b-7 - The bride becomes so consumed by ministry that she forsakes her first love. She falls into burnout and compromise. Finally, she cries out for Jesus to restore her to the place of intimacy.

<u>Season 2</u>: **Divine Identity bestowed 1 – 1:7 – 2:7** – The Bridegroom hears the cry of the bride and

invites her to follow Him again. As she responds, He imparts Divine Identity deep into her spirit.

Season 3: The invitation out of the comfort zone- 2:8-17 - Jesus comes as the overcoming King to invite the Bride to the place of partnership in arduous ministry and intercession. In verse 17, the bride in fear and immaturity rejects the Bridegroom's invitation.

Season 4: Divine Chastening – 3:1-5 – The Bridegroom does what the bride asks and leaves. As the bride realises her emptiness without His tangible presence she arises to search for Him.

Season 4a: Jesus as the safe leader – 3:6-11 – As the bride comes to search for Him, Jesus allows Himself to be found. In the experience of finding Him, Jesus reveals Himself as the passionate King, victorious intercessor and safe leader.

Season 5: Divine Identity bestowed 2 – 4:1-5 – The Bridegroom continues to affirm the budding character attributes He seems forming in the bride.

Season 5a: The bride accepts the Bridegroom's invitation – 4:6 – The bride, overwhelmed by the affirmation and love of Jesus, finally accepts His invitation to the place of arduous ministry as His inseparable partner.

Season 5b: **Jesus shares His beauty with the Bride** –4:7-15 – the Bridegroom reveals the beautiful character He is planting in the bride's heart through her journey.

Season 6: **The fellowship of His suffering** – 4:16-5:9 – As the bride invites Jesus to have all of her life He takes her into a season of testing. His question to her is: Am I enough? In the answering of this question Jesus draws His bride into a new depth of intimacy.

Season 6a: **The beauty of the King** –5:10-16 – The bride passes the test of love as she proclaims the incomparable beauty, worth and faithfulness of her Bridegroom King.

Season 7: **The fruit of responding rightly** –6:1-10 – By responding rightly in the time of testing, the bride sees immature believers provoked to search Him out. She also discovers she has greatly moved the Lord's heart and this time of testing has produced great maturity in her.

Season 7a: **The bride goes down to the harvest field** – 6:11-13 – Finally, the bride goes down to join the Bridegroom in His harvest field.

Season 8 - 7:1 – 9 – The Bridegroom fully possesses the beautiful, mature heart of the bride and completes the preparation of her heart for partnership.

Season 8a - 7:9 – 8:4 - The bride delights in the love of the Bridegroom.

Here ends the main part of the journey. Chapter 8:5-14 is a Coda [a concluding passage which often answers the question: what happens next?]

8:5a – A picture of the witness of the bride's deep dependence upon the Bridegroom [The end of the wilderness]

8:5b-7 – The bride proclaims the strength of their love as well as her assignment to intercede for Jesus' inheritance.

8:6-14 - The bride becomes a shepherd of other's hearts going on the journey of intimacy with Jesus and an intercessor crying out: Come, Lord Jesus come!

NOTE 2

A PARAPHRASE OF THE SONG OF SOLOMON

CHAPTER 1

¹The greatest song of all songs which was written by Solomon.

The Bride:

²Father God, I ask You that Your Son would touch my heart with His love through His Word, even as a kiss moves the heart of a lover. For the love of Your Son is better than any of the pleasures of this world.

³Your love gives me joy. Even the memory of Your love is like a fragrance that is intoxicating. The memory of Your love attracts me like the perfume of one that I love. Even in the very mention of Your name I find the memory of the times You touched my heart.

⁴ Oh King Jesus, let us run into ministry inseparably joined by our love.

The Daughters of Jerusalem:
We want to follow Jesus too.

The Bride:
Oh, Father, thank you for Your son, for He is kissing my soul with the revelation of His heart for me. He has answered my prayer and taken me away with Him to the secret place, to the intimate chamber to overwhelm me with His love.

(There is a long period of time in the story between these two sentences)

The Daughters of Jerusalem (proclaiming but perhaps not even knowing the full truth of what they are saying):
We will be glad and rejoice in Jesus.

We remember what you said oh Shulamite that the pleasure of His love is greater than the pleasures of this world.

The Bride after a long season of service, burn out and compromise:
Oh I remember too what it is to be loved by Him. I remember the secret place that He took me before. Rightly do the Daughters of Jerusalem love You my Beloved.

⁵I have become dark with sin in this season but I remember when You had me in the intimate place

how You called me lovely. I know Your heart! I know that You still call me lovely even now.

Now lamenting to the Daughters of Jerusalem: Oh daughters of Jerusalem, my sin is like the black tents of those who live in Kedar (Saudi Arabia) but truly I know that my Bridegroom has called me beautiful even as the curtains are in the temple of Solomon.

⁶Oh friends, do not look upon me, because I am stained black by my sin, the things of this world have burned me. The expectations of the church when I served her meant that my own heart I have neglected and it has turned to sin. My own heart has grown dull.

Turning back towards Jesus, the bride says:
⁷Tell me, my beloved Jesus, where is it that I can find again the intimacy that I once had with You? I don't want my heart to be ashamed anymore. I wish to rest where You are. I wish to have the intimacy that we used to have, that face to face, heart to heart intimacy.

Jesus:
⁸If you do not know where to find Me My beautiful one, follow in the footsteps of other faithful believers who have gone before you. You must follow the narrow path that is not easily found. It is a path like the tracks animals leave through the wilderness.

⁹My beautiful one, I have compared you to a great horse among all of Pharaoh's horses. You are the best of the best, the most beautiful of the most beautiful, you are truly unique to Me, you are My favourite one.

¹⁰Your emotions towards Me, your longing and love for Me will be perfect like golden ornaments. The posture of your heart, the humility of your surrender will be like the beauty of a gold chain around your head.

¹¹As we journey together My bride, I will array you with ornaments of gold (divine character) and earrings of silver (the testimony of redemption).

The Bride:

¹²When I place King Jesus in the rightful place in my life, my heart burns with love for Him.

¹³My heart suffers with longing for Him.

¹⁴Truly He is to me like the fragrance of flowers smelt in the desert when an Oasis is nearby.

Jesus:

¹⁵You are beautiful! Your devotion and longing for me are like the eyes of a dove which never waiver.

The Bride (responding to the delight of the Beloved):

¹⁶How handsome You are, Jesus, how beautiful are Your ways and Your Words. My love is inexperienced, I have so much still to learn. Help me.

¹⁷Yet, You have taken me away with You into Your palace which is secure and safe. There is such security and peace in Your love.

CHAPTER 2

¹I am a Rose of the desert, a flower that has lived in the darkness of the valley where light rarely comes.

Jesus:

²Yes you are right that you are a flower but you are so much more than a mere flower. You are a flower of such rare beauty that everything in comparison to you is as thorns and thistles.

The Bride:

³You are like an apple tree among the trees of the forest my Beloved. How rare to find such as You. I love to sit in Your presence because Your Words and Your love, the fruit of Your work on the cross, are as sweet as the sweetest apples to me.

The Bride speaking to the Daughters of Jerusalem:

⁴He has brought me into His house of abundance and lavished me with His love. His leadership concerning me is about cultivating my love for Him.

⁵He feeds me with both old and new revelations of His love. With both the old and new testament, with both the logos (the logical Word) and the rhema (heart revelation).

⁶I know that even when I can't see it, His left hand is under my head holding me. I know that His right arm, which is mighty to save, is around me and holding me safe.

⁷I challenge you, Daughters of Jerusalem, do not move onto the next season of intimacy with Jesus before the time is right. Stay here and do not move until Jesus moves. Stay close to Him at all times.

The Bride:

⁸Oh I hear the voice of my Beloved! What is this? He comes to me in a new way! I have never seen Him like this before. He comes from the place of difficult ministry, from hills and mountains where He leaps so easily.

⁹My Beloved makes those hard places, those frightening places look so easy the way He skips across them on His way to me. He comes for me.

¹⁰My Beloved spoke and said to me, "Rise up, my love, and come with me to the hills and mountains. Come and face the difficult places of ministry by My side.

¹¹See I am with you now and these places no longer need to be too hard and scary for you.

¹²It is time to conquer your fear of burnout, it is time to conquer these fears with My love.

¹³Rise up My love and come with Me. Let us face these places together.

¹⁴Don't hide from Me My love. Do not shrink away. Remember My love. If you are going to hide, hide in the cleft that was made in My side at the cross, hide in My love but let Me see your face and hear your voice for you are beautiful to me.

¹⁵Come on, let us catch those last little compromises in your life that hold you back from fully experiencing My love.

The Bride (speaking to Jesus):
¹⁶My Beloved is mine and I am His. I know that He satisfies the ones He loves with the finest of food.

¹⁷But my Beloved, I cannot go with You, there is still fear inside me. Go instead without me but leave me here.

CHAPTER 3

The Bride (now alone):
¹That night I was alone and my heart longed for my Beloved. I looked for Him in the palace but He

had gone. I looked for Jesus in the intimate chamber of the secret place but He had gone.

²Finally, I decided that I would go and search for Him. My desire was too strong. I could not resist. So I went to look. I looked but did not find Him.

³The watchmen of the church found me and I asked them, "Have you seen the One I love?" But they had not seen Him.

⁴Scarcely had the watchmen come out to help me than my Beloved appeared. It was as if He found me though it was I who was looking for Him. I held Him and would not let Him go. I would not let Him go! I wanted Him to come to the church, the church in which I first decided to follow Him.

⁵I advise you Daughters of Jerusalem, do not move onto the next season before the time is right. Stay here and do not move until Jesus moves. Stay close to Him at all times!

The Shulamite remembering the journey of her heart as her Beloved found her in the night at the mercy of the watchmen:

⁶Who is this coming out of the wilderness for me, like pillars of smoke on the horizon? He announces His coming. My Beloved is perfumed with myrrh and frankincense (He has interceded on my behalf and it has cost Him greatly). Who is this Man who would do such a thing for me?

⁷Behold! My Beloved comes up with sixty mighty angels at arms, the mighty ones of Israel. They come to protect me.

⁸They all carry weapons, they are trained from birth in the art of war, to protect against the terrors of the evil one.

⁹With them the King brings a couch. It is a palanquin which He has made Himself, for His queen.

¹⁰He has made its pillars of silver (redemption), its support of gold (divine character), its seat of purple (royalty). It is a ROYAL carriage in every regard, made with love by my carpenter of Nazareth, Jesus.

The Bride to the daughters of Jerusalem:

¹¹Go forth Daughters of Jerusalem and see Him. He is my Beloved, He is the King. One day He will be crowned by His Church and His bride in glory and splendour on the day of His wedding, on the day of His joy!

CHAPTER 4

Jesus, declaring prophetically what He sees in the bride:

¹Behold you are beautiful My love! Behold you are fair! Your eyes, like dove's eyes, are unwavering

in their pursuit and focus. Your hair is straight, the hair of Nazarite devotion.

²Your teeth are perfectly matched, perfectly prepared for chewing upon and digesting my Word.

³Your lips are like a strand of scarlet, your speech is redemptive. Your mouth is lovely, I love the intimacy I share with you. Your temples/cheeks/countenance, your emotions towards Me are beautiful.

⁴You have set your will to obey Me like David did. You will have an inheritance like David. You will be mighty in the Spiritual realm and many will come to you for protection.

⁵You are being equipped to nurture others.

The Bride:

⁶Oh my Beloved, I am overwhelmed by Your affirmation! Until the day breaks and the shadows flee away, until the dawn of the new age, now I will go with you wherever you go. I will go with you over the mountain of difficult ministry. I will go with you to the hill of burdensome intercession.

Jesus:

⁷You are perfectly beautiful my love. There is no blemish in you. I see you as you will be!

⁸Yes, come with Me from the resting place My bride. Come with Me to the mountains of Spiritual warfare. When we have conquered you will look across the land of your inheritance from the tops of

these very mountains which you thought were so hard before.

⁹You have stolen my heart completely My sister, My bride. You have stolen My heart with one look of your eyes, with your will to seek Me out.

¹⁰How beautiful is your love My sister, My bride! How pleasurable is your love! It is better than anything in the entire created universe.

¹¹Your speech, O My bride, the sweet words that you whisper to me in secret mean so much. I have washed you clean, your deeds are beautiful before me.

¹²Your heart is like a locked up garden My sister, My bride, for in this season I have closed you up for Myself. But look and see what I have done there, it is a spring of living water welling up to eternal life.

¹³,¹⁴Even in this locked up state, even though your heart has been hidden away for so long during your times of difficulty I have still been working in it. In your heart I have planted a beautiful garden. In the garden I have planted: righteousness and fruitfulness that impacts others (Pomegranates), the precious and costly sanctifying work of the Holy Spirit (Henna), the light of the gospel shining forth (spikenard), costly but triumphant faith (saffron), anointing in ministry (calamus and cinnamon), a lifestyle of prayer (frankincense), a revelation of the cross

and suffering as well as a willingness to surrender all for love (Myrrh and aloes).

¹⁵In your heart I have placed: a fountain (sensitivity to the Spirit), a well (a history in God) and a stream (an ability to pour out to others).

Bride:
¹⁶Oh my Beloved, Your work in my heart is beautiful. I am so overwhelmed to see what You have been doing inside of me even when I thought you were far off. You really can be trusted! I trust you! Whatever it takes, wherever the wind may blow I trust you. Beloved, come into my heart, let the beauty of this garden You have planted be seen by all for Your glory!

CHAPTER 5

Jesus:
¹I have come to take full possession of your heart, my sister (I love you like family) and my bride (I love you as my spouse, Ephesians 5:28). I have enjoyed your heart, I have enjoyed the fragrance of your relentless pursuit of me even through difficulty, the fragrance of My grace is sweet upon you. Your life and the fruit of your life is as sweet as honey to My

taste, I celebrate your maturity and your strength in Me.

Turning to the Father and Holy Spirit Jesus says: Eat, O Friends! Let us celebrate the purity of My bride, the perfection of My bride. Drink, yes, drink deeply in celebration, O Beloved Ones!

The Bride:

²I slept and rested with confidence in my Beloved (the rest of faith, Matthew 8:23-27). Even though I was asleep, my heart was awakened to the voice of my Beloved. Jesus called to me saying, "Open your heart for me, my sister (I love you like family), my love (you are the apple of my eye), my dove (my devoted/pure one), my perfect one. Open your heart for me to share with you the burdens of my heart. My hair is covered with dew for I have been in the garden of Gethsemane, on the hill of intercession for my inheritance (lost souls). Now is the time for you to come and be with Me on the mountain of myrrh and the hill of frankincense. I want to take you. Will you open your heart for Me to share the burdens of My heart with you? Will you come on this new journey with Me?"

The Bride responds:

³(Rhetorical question) How can I refuse my Beloved? I have refused once, I have strayed from You before and I will not refuse You or stray again.

⁴My Beloved turned the handle of the door to my heart but stopped and my heart longed for Him.

⁵I arose from my place of peaceful rest to open the door of my heart for Him. My hands dripped with the longing of my Beloved for lost souls which He had left on the handle of the door of my heart.

⁶I opened my heart but His tangible presence was gone. What is this new place He wants to take me I wondered? I sought Him but I could not find him. I called for Him, but He gave me no answer. I went out into the night and onto the street knowing that I would find him in His harvest field.

⁷The watchmen of the church found me again. This time they were confused as to why I was searching again for my beloved. They did not have mercy on me. They beat me and they wounded me. They took away my veil (my ministry), they humiliated me.

⁸Yet my heart is focused on one thing and one thing only. I charge you, O daughters of Jerusalem, if you find my Beloved Jesus, tell Him that I am lovesick for Him! I don't care about the beating, the wounding or the humiliation. I don't care that I lost my ministry. I care about finding my Beloved and being with Him where He is!

The daughters of Jerusalem:

⁹What?! We don't understand?! Who is your Beloved that even though you have been beaten your heart is still fixed on Him, on this One thing? How is it that, though He has allowed you out into the night to be beaten, you still long for Him? How is it that you still love Him? How is it that you still desire Him? Tell us about Him? Who is this One that you love?

The Bride:

¹⁰My Beloved is white and ruddy. My Beloved is both God and man. He is perfectly God and perfectly human. He was God but He humbled himself and took on humanity for our sake. I know that because of His experience as a man He knows how to lead me best. This is why I can trust Him. I know that He can identify with me and I know that out of that identification He can heal me of any wound I might bear. I trust that if I look upon His countenance everything will be ok. There is no one like him! There is no one like him!!

¹¹His leadership is perfect, refined over the ages, He knows how to lead me. He knows how to lead me better than I know how to lead myself. He knows because He created me and He knows my inward being. His devotion to me is like the devotion of a Nazarite. He is committed to me even unto death, even unto humiliation for He died on a tree for me.

¹²His eyes upon me are intent and unwavering. They see clearly. They see rightly. His judgements are perfect because His sight is perfect.

¹³He feels deep emotion towards me, great passion and longing, great love, great pleasure and enjoyment and great sorrow when I fall. His thoughts and Words about me outnumber the sand on the sea shore. His Words to me exhort me to embrace death to self.

¹⁴The work of His hands in my life is perfect, He is never slow, never too hasty in His actions. He never forgets to do something that needs to be done. His heart is like precious ivory inlaid with sapphires, it is a beautiful treasure!

¹⁵His ways are perfect and they can be trusted. I can trust that they will produce in me divine character and mature love. I can trust that they are based on His own divine character. His face is noble and good. Seeing His face reassures me of everything that He is.

¹⁶The kisses of His Word to my heart are the sweetest experience of my life. Yes, He is altogether lovely! This is my Beloved, this is my friend, O Daughters of Jerusalem!

The Song Jesus Sings

CHAPTER 6

The daughters of Jerusalem:

¹ Where has your beloved gone, O most beautiful among women? Where has your beloved turned, that we may seek him with you?

The Bride:

²My Beloved has gone to His garden, He has gone down to feed his flock, He has gone to tend to the other ones who He is teaching about His love.

³I am my Beloved's, and my Beloved is mine. It is good and right that He feeds his flock, that He tends to His harvest field!

Jesus (comes to his bride):

⁴You have passed the test! O my love, outwardly you are beautiful. Inwardly you are stunning, your heart is beautiful. You have triumphed and your victory is like a conquering army coming home from battle and raising its banners of victory!

⁵Your love and devotion overwhelm Me. Your devotion to Me is like that of a Nazarite.

⁶Your teeth, your ability to chew on the Word, is well developed.

⁷Your emotions, even in the time of testing, are like Mine.

⁸There are many in my court who are followers of Me, who are servants of Mine.

⁹But My devoted one, My perfect one, you are unique. There is no one like you. You are my favourite one.

¹⁰Who is this who brings forth great hope for others in her countenance, who brings forth beauty in dark times (see Psalm 84:5-7), dazzling glory in good times? Your triumph is a testimony for all to see!

The Bride:

¹¹I went down to the orchard of my Beloved. I went down to see the green plants of the valley. I went down to see whether the vines has sprouted, whether the pomegranates had brought forth flowers yet, whether the inheritance of my Beloved was coming forth, whether the harvest field was ripe for the harvest.

¹²Before I was even aware, to my surprise, my desire for my Beloved's inheritance was strong within me and before I even knew what I was doing I was amongst my Beloved's inheritance, working diligently with my hands and all my heart.

¹³I was so shocked and surprised by my desire, by this new desire to be with ones who had not really trusted me in the past, that I stood up to leave but they called to me: "Return, return, O Shulamite, that we may look upon you and learn from you." But I said, "Why is it that you want to look upon me?" I remembered the way they had left me at the mercy

of the watchmen previously and I wondered in my head why suddenly my heart loved them, how suddenly I could love them.

CHAPTER 7

Jesus (proclaiming over the Bride):
¹How beautiful are your feet that bring the good news of the gospel to everyone you meet, my beautiful bride! The curve of your thighs, the elegance of your walk of obedience with me is the work of the hands of a skilful workman.

²,³Your ability to nurture others into the deep things of the faith is well prepared for the season that is to come.

⁴The yielding of your will to mine is complete and perfect. Your spiritual eyes are clear in what they see and perceive. Their sight is deep in wisdom like the pools of Heshbon by the gate of Bath Rabbim. Your insight is also well formed. Like a watch tower you can see into deep things and also things afar off.

⁵Your thoughts towards me crown you and define you as royalty. A King is held captive by your beauty!

⁶, ⁷, ⁸How beautiful you are, My bride! This character of yours is without flaw. I will come now again and delight in your presence.

The Bride:

⁹The wine of your love is sweet again to my taste, my Lord and King! I belong to my Bridegroom and I know for sure that His desire is for me.

¹⁰, ¹¹, ¹²Come my Bridegroom, let us go into the harvest field. Let us go to see the growing of Your inheritance in the vineyard. Let us go to see how it grows. Let us go to tend it together.

¹³My love for you gives off a fragrance to all around. This is my testimony, this is my proclamation in the harvest field.

Chapter 8

¹O how I long to bring You, my Beloved Jesus, into the church and share You with those in the place of my spiritual birth.

²There our journey of love, and the holiness it has produced in my life, would be a testimony about the worth of who You are Jesus. Would that not please You?

Turning and speaking to the daughters of Jerusalem:

³But though the time for that is not yet, I know He is still leading me well! I know that His left hand

is still under my head and His mighty right arm is still holding me close.

⁴Daughters of Jerusalem, I advise you, stay in the season He has you. He will lead you on when the time is right!

A relative seeing the bride says:
⁵Who is this coming up from the wilderness leaning, trusting her Beloved so completely?!

The bride:
Now in the place of intimacy, under the apple tree, I will awaken Your heart, Jesus, through intercession for the lost. In that same place of intimate intercession someone in my church awakened You on my behalf and now I will do the same for others!

⁶O Jesus, set me as a seal upon Your heart, as a seal upon Your arm. Do not let our love ever fail because my love for You is as strong as death, my jealousy for You were You to depart would be as cruel as death.

⁷Nothing, not even a tidal wave, could quench my love for You now. Even if all the wealth in the world were given to buy my love I would see that wealth as utterly worthless.

The Church members:
⁸Beautiful bride, we have a little sister who wants to go on the same journey as you yet she is young and immature. Where shall we direct her?

The bride:

⁹If she is an intercessor (wall – Isaiah 62:6) I would build in her a deep revelation regarding the beauty of her salvation. If she is an evangelist (door – John 10:3) I would direct her into the secret place to hear the heart of the Bridegroom.

The bride's final declaration:

¹⁰I am an intercessor and the heart of longing I have to nurture others is as deep as a tower is high. But I have found peace in the locked gaze of intimacy with my Beloved one. It is from the place of intimacy that we will work together.

¹¹King Jesus has a vineyard made up of multitudes (the Church). It's keepers (the shepherds of the Church) know that they have been charged to be faithful with what He has entrusted to them.

¹²I also will be faithful with the vineyard (large or small) You have given me for it is a great joy to me.

The Daughters of Jerusalem:

¹³We in the vineyards listen for Your voice, Jesus, our Bridegroom.

The Daughters of Jerusalem and the Bride together:

¹⁴Make haste and come quickly Lord Jesus. Come in response to the deep yearning of Your people. The Spirit and the Bride say, "Come!"

NOTE 3

....

UNDERSTANDING THE LANGUAGE OF THE SONG OF SONGS

Song 1:2	**Mouth** The word of God Deuteronomy 8:3
Song 1:2	**Wine** The pleasures of this world, even legiti-mate pleasures Psalm 63:3; Psalm 16:11; Psalm 104:15
Song 1:3	**Fragrance** Fragrance – a smell 2 Corinthians 2:14-16

UNDERSTANDING THE LANGUAGE OF THE SONG OF SONGS

Song 1:3	**Ointment**	
	A perfume with a pleasing fragrance	
	2 Corinthians 2:14-16; John 12:1-8	
Song 1:4	**Chambers**	
	The intimate place where hearts are shared	
	1 Chronicles 28:11	
Song 1:5	**Dark**	
	Sinful	
	1 John 1:6	
Song 1:5	**Kedar**	
	Arabia	
	Ezekiel 27:21	
Song 1:6	**Sun**	
	The world (Concluded by observing that it is the sun that causes the bride to be burnt and darkened with sin)	
	Mark 4:6	
Song 1:6	**Mother**	
	The church/the one who gave you spiritual birth	
	Galatians 4:26-28; 1 Thessalonians 2:7	

The Song Jesus Sings

Song 1:6	**Mother's sons**
	Those in the institutional church
	Galatians 4:26-28
Song 1:6	**Vineyard**
	The inner life of the believer
	John 15:1-7
Song 1:7	**Flock**
	Disciples
	John 10:14-16
Song 1:7	**Veil's herself**
	Hides herself because she is a stranger. In Hebrew culture a woman who was amongst strangers would veil herself.
Song 1:8	**Follow in the footsteps of the flock**
	Follow in the narrow path of lovers of Jesus who have gone before.
	Matthew 7:13-14; Jeremiah 6:16
Song 1:8	**Little goats**
	Your own disciples

Song 1:9	**Pharaoh's chariot** The horses of Egypt were the very best horses and therefore the horse that pulled Pharaoh's chariot would have been the very best of the best. 1 Kings 10:28
Song 1:9	**Filly** Mare/female horse
Song 1:10	**Cheeks** Strong emotions (think of blushing)
Song 1:10	**Ornaments** Made beautiful for God 1 Peter 3:3-4; 1 Samuel 16:7; Galatians 5:22
Song 1:10	**Neck** A person's will Exodus 32:9; Isaiah 3:16
Song 1:11	**Gold** Divine character Galatians 5:22; 1 Peter 3:3-4;

Song 1:11	**Silver** Redemption Exodus 21:32; Matthew 26:15
Song 1:12	**Spikenard/nard** A costly anointing oil, for anointing acts of consecration, dedication and worship, in Hebrew it means 'light'. In Greek it means genuine and pure. In Song of Songs 1:12, the King is sitting, which is symbolic of His finished work at Calvary's tree. He is inviting her to come and join Him at the marriage supper feast. The bride's fragrance emanates out of her spirit in worship and adoration for the King's provision. This is a heavenly fragrance we should all possess. John 12:3; Mark 14:3-9
Song 1:13	**Myrrh** The pain of longing (Messianic prophecy - Psalm 45:8; One of the oils that Jesus was buried in: Matthew 2:11; John 19:39) Proverbs 7:17; Exodus 30:23; Mark 15:23

Song 1:13	**A bundle of myrrh**
	An ancient form of perfume was to sleep with a packet of fragrant spice hung around ones neck. By morning the fragrance had permeated your skin and hair leaving you smelling of it for the remainder of the day.
	2 Corinthians 2:14-16
Song 1:14	**Henna blooms**
	From the Hebrew root kofer meaning ransom. Henna here signifies the precious and costly sanctifying work of the Holy Spirit
	Exodus 21:30; Exodus 30:12; Numbers 35:31; Numbers 35:32; Job 36:18; Psalm 49:7; Proverbs 13:8
Song 1:14	**En Gedi**
	An oasis in the desert
Song 1:15	**Dove's eyes**
	Eyes of devotion. A dove must move its whole head if it wants to look at you. A person with dove's eyes is one who is unwavering in their pursuit of Jesus. Doves

also only have one mate through their entire lives. This speaks of our fidelity to Jesus.
Matthew 6:22, 23

Song 1:16	**Our bed is green** Our love is new, fresh and flourishing.
Song 1:17	**Cedar and firs** A house build of cedars and firs would be solid and safe, built by the strongest, most valuable timber available at the time. 1 Kings 5:10
Song 2:1	**Rose of Sharon** A beautiful flower found in the hills of Israel
Song 2:2	**Lily among thorns** Purity that stands out amongst all the rest
Song 2:3	**Apple tree** The cross 1 Peter 2:25

Song 2:3	**His fruit** The fruit of Jesus' work on the cross 1 Peter 2:25
Song 2:4	**Banqueting house** Hebrew: The house of wine. The place of delight that comes from encountering the beauty of God's heart. Deuteronomy 8: 3
Song 2:4	**Banner** leadership Numbers 10:14, 18, 22, 25
Song 2:5	**Cakes of raisins** Old testament – Dried/old fruit Matthew 13:52
Song 2:5	**Apples** New testament – Fresh fruit Matthew 13:52
Song 2:6	**His left hand** His leadership that I cannot perceive but is still there

Song 2:6	**His right hand** The mighty right arm of the Lord, His strength and power working visibly on my behalf Exodus 15:6; Psalm 63:8; Psalm 89:13; Psalm 108:6; Isaiah 41:10
Song 2:7	**Gazelles and does of the field** Deer and gazelle are symbols of the joys of love
Song 2:8	**Mountains and hills** Hardships and difficulties Mark 11:23; Zechariah 4:7
Song 2:9	**Gazelle or young stag** Young and strong Psalm 18:33; Habakkuk 3:19
Song 2:9	**Wall and lattice** Jesus is coming to the secret places of the bride's heart
Song 2:11	**The winter and the rain** "The season is changing, the time of emptiness is ending. Even on the

mountains and hills, those places that are difficult, I will be close to you," says the Bridegroom.

Song 2:14	**Clefts of the rock** The hiding place Exodus 33:20-22
Song 2:15	**The foxes** The little compromises in the life of the bride
Song 2:15	**Vines** The inner life of the believer John 15
Song 2:16	**Lillies** Purity 1 Kings 7:19
Song 2:17	**Day breaks and shadows flee away** Until dawn, until I can overcome my fear
Song 2:17	**Bether** The Hebrew meaning of the word Bether is Separation/divide Genesis 15:10

Song 3:3	**The watchmen** Hebrew: The keepers. Symbolises the leaders/gatekeepers of the church Hebrews 13:17
Song 3:4	**Mother** The church/the one in which you were birthed spiritually Galatians 4:26-28
Song 3:6	**Pillars of smoke** The presence of God, majestic like the pillar of cloud and fire that led the Israelites through the wilderness Exodus 13:21; Ezekiel 1:4
Song 3:6	**Myrrh** The cross, suffering and death to self (Messianic prophecy - Psalm 45:8; One of the oils that Jesus was buried in: Matthew 2:11; John 19:39) Proverbs 7:17; Exodus 30:23; Mark 15:23
Song 3:6	**Frankincense** A lifestyle of prayer Exodus 30: 34-38; Leviticus 2; Leviticus 6:15

Song 3:6	**Merchants fragrant powders**
	The merchant's powders speak of Jesus' commitment to us. Jesus spoke of merchants who sold everything to purchase beautiful pearls (His Bride). A merchant was scented as a result of handling (buying and selling) the perfumed powders in the marketplace. Jesus is the perfumed merchant who sold everything in His deep commitment to us.
	Matthew 13:45, 46
Song 3:7	**Couch/Bed**
	A covered, portable couch carried by servants – the secret place of intimacy and union.
Song 3:7	**Valiant men**
	Warrior angels
	Psalm 91:11
Song 3:8	**Fear in the night**
	Flaming arrows of the evil one
	Psalm 91:5
Song 3:9	**Wood of Lebanon**
	The finest wood available

The Song Jesus Sings

1 Kings 5:10

Song 3:9	**Palanquin** A covered, portable throne or couch carried by servants Ephesians 1:20-21
Song 3:10	**Silver** Redemption Exodus 21:32; Matthew 26:15
Song 3:10	**Gold** Divine character Galatians 5:22; 1 Peter 3:3-4;
Song 3:10	**Purple** Of royal/divine birth Exodus 36:35; 2 Chronicles 3:14;
Song 3:11	**Daughters of Zion** The cloud of witnesses Zechariah 9:9
Song 3:11	**The day of the gladness of his heart** Jesus' wedding day Isaiah 62:5

Song 4:1	**Dove's eyes** Eyes of devotion. A dove must move its whole head if it wants to look at you. A person with dove's eyes is one who is un-wavering in their pursuit of Jesus. Doves also only have one mate through their entire lives. This speaks of our fidelity to Jesus. Matthew 6:22, 23
Song 4:1	**Hair like a flock of goats** Nazarite consecration Numbers 6:1-21
Song 4:2	**Teeth** One's ability to chew on the word of God, to understand it and meditate on it 1 Corinthians 3:1-2; Hebrews 5:12-14
Song 4:3	**Lips** The bride's speech Ephesians 4:29; James 2:3
Song 4:3	**Mouth** Intimacy that the bride and Bridegroom share Song of Songs 1:2

The Song Jesus Sings

Song 4:3	**Temples (the same as cheeks)**
	A person's emotions are righteous
	Psalm 4:4
Song 4:3	**Pomegranates**
	In the Jewish tradition the pomegranate is a sacred fruit used as a symbol of righteousness because a pomegranate is believed to have 613 seeds which correspond to the 613 commandments of the Torah. Righteousness, fruitfulness, learning, knowledge, wisdom (http://www.jewishgiftplace.com/Symbolism-Of-Pomegranate.html)
	(Exodus 28:33-34; Exodus 39: 24-26; 1 Kings 7:13-22; 1 Kings 7:42; 2 Kings 25:17; 2 Chronicles 3:16; 2 Chronicles 4:13)
Song 4:4	**Neck**
	A person's will (e.g. stiff-necked)
	Exodus 32:9; Isaiah 3:16
Song 4:4	**Tower of David**
	Established by many victories of surrender and obedience to Jesus

Song 4:5	**Breasts**	
	Ability to nurture others	
Song 4:6	**Myrrh**	
	the cross, suffering and death to self (Messianic prophecy - Psalm 45:8; One of the oils that Jesus was buried in: Matthew 2:11; John 19:39) Proverbs 7:17; Exodus 30:23; Mark 15:23	
Song 4:6	**Frankincense**	
	A lifestyle of prayer	
	Exodus 30: 34-38; Leviticus 2; Leviticus 6:15	
Song 4:7	**No spot**	
	No sin	
	Ephesians 5:27	
Song 4:8	**Lebanon**	
	The place where King Solomon had his holiday palace. The place of intimacy, the King's chamber, the place sitting under the apple tree.	

Song 4:8	**Amana, Senir, Hermon** Mountains on the border of Lebanon and Israel. The mountains spoken of in Ch. 2:8.
Song 4:8	**Lions' dens, mountains of the leopards** The places of difficulty Habakuk 2:17
Song 4:9	**Ravished** Dictionary definition: To be filled with strong emotion, especially joy
Song 4:9	**Spouse** Bride/wife-to-be
Song 4:9	**Link of your necklace** Act of obedience Song of Songs 1:10
Song 4:10	**Wine** Anything this world has to offer Song of Songs 1:2; Psalm 63:3; Psalm 16:11
Song 4:10	**Perfumes** The testimony of the revelation of God in our lives (See Value 6)

2 Corinthians 2:14-16; John 12:1-8

Song 4:11	**Lips**
	Your words/prayers to me
	Ephesians 4:29; James 2:3
Song 4:11	**Honeycomb**
	Sweetness
	Psalm 19:10
Song 4:11	**Honey and milk**
	Sweetness and purity
Song 4:11	**Fragrance**
	The testimony of the revelation of God in our lives (See Value 6)
	2 Corinthians 2:14-16
Song 4:11	**Fragrance of Lebanon**
	Fragrance that can only come from the intimate place
	Revelation 19:7-8
Song 4:12	**Garden**
	The heart

Song 4:12	**Spring/fountain** The heart – the wellspring of life Proverbs 4:23; John 4:14
Song 4:13	**Plants** The fruit that is in your heart Galatians 5:22, 23;
Song 4:13	**Pomegranates** In the Jewish tradition the pomegranate is a sacred fruit used as a symbol of righteousness because a pomegranate is believed to have 613 seeds which correspond to the 613 commandments of the Torah. Righteousness, fruitfulness, learning, knowledge, wisdom (http://www.jewishgiftplace.com/Symbolism-Of-Pomegranate.html) Exodus 28:33-34; Exodus 39: 24-26; 1 Kings 7:13-22; 1 Kings 7:42; 2 Kings 25:17; 2 Chronicles 3:16; 2 Chronicles 4:13
Song 4:13	**Henna** The precious and costly sanctifying work of the Holy Spirit. The root word in Hebrew for Henna is 'Kofer', this word has a dual meaning. It can also mean the

price of atonement. For example, Isaiah 43:3 says, "For I am the Lord your God, the Holy one of Israel, your Saviour; I gave Egypt for your ransom [Kofer], Ethiopia and Seba in your place."
Exodus 21:30; Exodus 30:12; Numbers 35:31; Numbers 35:32; Job 36:18; Psalm 49:7; Proverbs 13:8

Song 4:14 **Spikenard**

A costly anointing oil, for anointing acts of consecration, dedication and worship, in Hebrew it means 'light'. In Greek it means genuine and pure. In Song of Songs 1:12, the King is sitting, which is symbolic of His finished work at Calvary's tree. He is inviting her to come and join Him at the marriage supper feast. The bride's fragrance emanates out of her spirit in worship and adoration for the King's provision. This is a heavenly fragrance we should all possess.
John 12:3; Mark 14:3-9

Song 4:14 **Saffron**

Saffron is only ever mentioned in the Bible in this passage of Song of Songs.

However, Saffron is a very expensive spice from an orange-yellow flower of the crocus family. It is literally worth its weight in gold because it is the stigmas from which the spice is obtained. Each one is handpicked and placed over a charcoal fire for drying. It takes over 75,000 flowers to make one pound of saffron.

Saffron is said to symbolize the costly but triumphant faith of the Messiah against His enemy. Believers can live by faith just as the disciples did, knowing that the testing of their faith through fire will be more precious than gold. 1 Peter 1:7-8 (http://www.rebeccatotilo.com/spiritual-significance-of-saffron/)

Song 4:14	**Calamus**

A key ingredient of Holy anointing oil (Exodus 30:22-33). This word has a dual meaning. It can mean the Calamus plant as described here in Song of Songs or it can also mean: reed or rod, something used for measuring. It speaks of the beauty of holiness.

Ezekiel 29:6; Ezekiel 40:3, 5, 6, 8; Ezekiel 41:8; Ezekiel 42:16-19

Song 4:14 **Cinnamon**
A key ingredient of Holy anointing oil. Set apart for God.
Exodus 30: 22-33

Song 4:14 **Myrrh**
The cross, suffering and death to self (Messianic prophecy - Psalm 45:8; One of the oils that Jesus was buried in: Matthew 2:11; John 19:39) Proverbs 7:17; Exodus 30:23; Mark 15:23

Song 4:14 **Aloes**
There are two plants referred to as "aloes" in the Bible. One is a rich, fragrant resin formed in the heartwood of the aquilaria tree, in response to a natural parasite, fungal, or mold attack. Burying the logs, the outer part decays while the inner, saturates with this resin. The tree may also be deliberately wounded to make it susceptible to attack. Thus, the fungus and decomposition process can take over several hundred years to

The Song Jesus Sings

produce, making it one of the most rare and expensive oils. The wounding of the "heartwood" of the tree.

In Isaiah 53:5, Isaiah prophesied of the Messiah's crucifixion, saying, "But he [was] wounded for our transgressions, [he was] bruised for our iniquities: the chastisement of our peace [was] upon him; and with his stripes we are healed."

Deliberately wounded for our disobedience of the law, Jesus took our punishment so that we could be reconciled to God and walk again in the fullness of life.

Messianic prophecy - Psalm 45:8; One of the oils that Jesus was embalmed in for burial – John 19:39

Song 4:15 — **Fountain, garden, well, streams**
The inner life
John 4:14

Song 4:16 — **North wind**
The rough cold wind of adversity

Song 4:16	**South wind**	
	The cool, south wind of blessing	
Song 4:16	**Spices**	
	Rich, expensive and beautiful gifts	
	2 Kings 10:2; Matthew 2:11	
Song 4:16	**Garden**	
	Our inner life in God	
	Proverbs 4:23	
Song 4:16	**Pleasant fruits**	
	The fruit of the spirit	
	Galatians 5:22, 23	
Song 5:1	**Myrrh, spice, honeycomb, honey, wine and milk**	
	The fruit stored up in the heart of the bride	
Song 5:1	**Friends**	
	The Father and Holy Spirit	
Song 5:1	**Drink**	
	Celebration	

Song 5:2	**Door** The door of my heart, the gateway to new revelation of the beauty of Jesus Revelation 3:20
Song 5:5	**Myrrh** The suffering that comes from longing and desire (Messianic prophecy - Psalm 45:8; One of the oils that Jesus was buried in: Matthew 2:11; John 19:39) Proverbs 7:17; Exodus 30:23; Mark 15:23
Song 5:7	**Watchmen** Hebrew definition: The keepers. Symbolises the leaders/gatekeepers of the institutional church Hebrews 13:17; Acts 20:28; 1 Peter 5:2-3
Song 5:7	**Veil** The Bride's ministry
Song 5:10	**White** Radiant with the light of God/divine nature Revelation 1:14; Matthew 7:2

Song 5:10	**Ruddy** Human nature Psalm 45:2
Song 5:11	**Head** Leadership Colossians 1:18; Ephesians 1:21-23
Song 5:11	**Gold** Divine/perfect Galatians 5:22; 1 Peter 3:3-4;
Song 5:11	**His locks are wavy and black as a raven** His devotion is like that of a nazarite who does not cut his hair. Numbers 6:1-21
Song 5:12	**His eyes are like doves by the rivers of waters, washed with milk and fitly set** His eyes do not leave me but he sees me perfectly as I truly am and will be Hebrews 4:13
Song 5:13	**His cheeks are like a bed of spices, banks of scented herbs** His emotions towards me are many Psalm 139:17, 18; Psalm 40:5

Song 5:13	**His lips are lilies dripping with liquid myrrh** Lips refer to His speech or His prayers for the bride. He always lives to intercede for me at the right hand of the Father and that intercession sounds something like this: "Father, I desire!" Hebrews 7:25
Song 5:14	**His hands (arms) are rods of gold set with beryl** The work of His hands in my life is perfect. Psalm 63:8; Psalm 89:13; Psalm 108:6; Isaiah 41:10;
Song 5:14	**His body is carved ivory inlaid with sapphires** His heart, the very core of His being, is full of beautiful thoughts, emotions and plans toward me.
Song 5:15	**His legs are pillars of marble set on bases of fine gold.** His way, His walk is perfect, He can be trusted. I can trust that He will produce in me divine character and mature love.

Song 5:15	**His countenance is like Lebanon excellent as cedars** His face has such love and affection on it towards me Psalm 4:6; Numbers 6:24-26
Song 5:16	**His mouth is most sweet** The kiss of His word to my heart is the sweetest experience of my life Song of Songs 1:2
Song 6:2	**Garden** The harvest field Isaiah 61:11; Matthew 13:3-9
Song 6:2	**Beds of spices** Represents diversity of expression within the church. Jesus loves the whole Church in all its various expressions.
Song 6:4	**Tirzah** Samariah – the capital of the northern Kingdom of Israel – Outward beauty. 1 Kings15:33

Song 6:4	**Jerusalem** Jerusalem – the capital of the southern Kingdom of Judah – Inward spiritual beauty. Psalm 48:2; Psalm 50:2; Revelation 21:2
Song 6:4	**An army with banners** Like a victorious army Zechariah 9:16, 17; Revelation 19:14-16
Song 6:5	**Hair** Nazarite consecration and devotion Numbers 6:1-21
Song 6:6	**Teeth** Ability to digest the word of God Hebrews 5:12-14
Song 6:7	**Temples** Emotions
Song 6:7	**Pomegranates** Righteousness

Song 6:7	**Like a piece of pomegranate are your temples behind your veil**
	Your righteousness and love for God is hidden in the secret place where God esteems it. The bride lives for an audience of One.
	Matthew 6:1-18
Song 6:8	**Queens and concubines**
	Other believers
	Psalm 45:9
Song 6:11	**Garden of nuts**
	The place where new Christians are birthed
	Isaiah 61:11; Matthew 13:3-9
Song 6:11	**Verdure of the valley; budding vine; pomegranates**
	Verdure means: fresh, flourishing vegetation.
	The new believers who would follow in the footsteps of the bride
	Isaiah 61:11; Matthew 13:3-9; Isaiah 5; John 15:1-7

Song 6:12	**My soul had made me as the chariots of my noble people** My heart was moved towards these ones who would soon be the inheritance of my beloved
Song 6:13	**Camps/armies/Mahanaim** The difference between those who are on the journey into intimacy and those who are not Genesis 32:1, 2
Song 7:1	**Feet** The feet that bring good news Isaiah 52:7
Song 7:1	**Thighs** Your walk of faith with Jesus
Song 7:2, 3	**Navel, waist, breasts** Ability to nurture and disciple others
Song 7:4	**Neck** The yielding of the will to Jesus Exodus 32:9; Isaiah 3:16; James 4:7

Song 7:4	**Your eyes like the pools in Heshbon** Ability to receive divine revelation Ephesians 1:18
Song 7:4	**Your nose is like the tower of Lebanon** The nose here represents the bride's ability to discern spiritually. A tower gives protection to a city. The bride has discernment against her fiercest enemies.
Song 7:5	**Your head crowns you like Mount Carmel** The bride's thought life is full of beautiful thoughts toward the Bridegroom Isaiah 35:2
Song 7:5	**The hair of your head is like purple** The devotion of a Nazarite which similar to the devotion of her King and bridegroom Jesus. Numbers 6:1-21
Song 7:5	**Tresses** Your dress Revelation 19:8

Song 7:8	**Breath like apples** Breath speaks of one's inner life. Apples speaks of refreshment. The inner life of the bride brings forth the refreshment of the Holy Spirit to others. John 20:22; Song of Songs 2:3
Song 7:9	**Roof of your mouth** Palate of the mouth, the words which the bride speaks bring the greatest joy to Jesus. Hebrews 13:15; Proverbs 16:24
Song 7:9	**Wine** Joy and pleasure of love imparted by the Holy Spirit Ephesians 5:18
Song 7:11, 12	**Field, villages, vineyards** The harvest field Isaiah 61:11; Matthew 13:3-9;
Song 7:12	**Vine, grape blossoms, pomegranates** The new believers who would follow in the footsteps of the bride Isaiah 61:11; Matthew 13:3-9; Isaiah 5; John 15:1-7

Song 7:13	**Mandrakes** A plant thought to improve fertility – the bride's love for the groom Genesis 30:14-16
Song 7:13	**Fruits** The fruit of the spirit Galatians 5:22, 23
Song 8:1	**Brother** Other believers in the Church Galatians 4:26-28
Song 8:1	**Mother's breasts** The discipleship and spiritual nurture offered by the true Church Galatians 4:26-28; 1 Thessalonians 2:7
Song 8:2	**The house of my mother** Jesus' true Church Galatians 4:26-28
Song 8:2	**Spiced wine, juice of my pomegranate** The love that the bride has for Jesus Song of Songs 1:2;

The Song Jesus Sings

Song 8:3   **Left hand**
          Invisible hand

Song 8:4   **Right hand**
          Mighty right arm
          Exodus 15:6; Psalm 63:8; Psalm 89:13; Psalm 108:6; Isaiah 41:10;

Song 8:5   **Apple tree**
          The place of intimacy
          Song of Songs 1:2; Song of Songs 2:3; 1 Peter 2:25

Song 8:5   **Your mother**
          Jesus' Church
          Galatians 4:26-28

Song 8:8   **No breasts**
          A potential bride who is not yet mature
          1 Corinthians 3:1, 2; Ezekiel 16:7

Song 8:9   **Wall**
          Intercessor
          Isaiah 62: 6, 7; Ezekiel 22:30

Song 8:9	**Battlement of silver**	
	A deep revelation of redemption	
	Exodus 21:32; Matthew 26:15	

Song 8:9	**Door**
	Evangelist
	Colossians 4:3

Song 8:9	**Cedar**
	Precious, hard, protective wood
	1 Kings 5:10

Song 8:10	**Breasts**
	Ability to nurture/disciple

Song 8:11	**Vineyard**
	A body of believers
	Matthew 21:33-43

Song 8:11	**Baal Hamon**
	The Lord of the multitude

Song 8:14	**Mountain of spices**
	The prayers of the saints/bride
	Revelation 5:8

ABOUT THE AUTHOR

Joel Ratcliffe lives in Sydney where he has helped to plant a House of Prayer and works in the publishing industry. His heart and irrevocable call is to see day and night prayer established in Australia unto the church prepared for the return of the Jesus. He writes a popular blog at chasingthebeautifulGod.com

www.ingramcontent.com/pod-product-compliance
Lightning Source LLC
Chambersburg PA
CBHW020417010526
44118CB00010B/297